The

CHURCH

and the

DARK
AGES

(430-1027)

"The so-called Dark Ages engenders images of a bloody, barbaric, and illiterate age without the light of civilization and progress. *The Church and the Dark Ages (430–1027)* refutes this erroneous notion, illustrating a time period of monasteries, missionaries, reform, and renewal. Phillip Campbell's worthy addition to the Reclaiming Catholic History series presents the five hundred years from the end of the classical age to the beginnings of the high Middle Ages in a compelling and positive light. The story of the Church is expertly told in an engaging manner and is a necessary addition to every Catholic home."

Steve Weidenkopf
Author of *The Church and the Middle Ages (1000–1378)*

"The Reclaiming Catholic History series is a boon and a blessing. It allows us to remember the past in an age of amnesia. Phillip Campbell's volume in this splendid series on the so-called Dark Ages shows us that they were anything but dark, but were instead the very dawn of Christendom, heralding the civilization of the Risen Son."

Joseph Pearce
Editor of *St. Austin Review*

"Engaging, instructive, and eminently enjoyable. Phillip Campbell sheds a bright light on the Dark Ages, exposing many of the myths that still cling to the centuries following the fall of the Western Roman Empire. From the death of St. Augustine in 430 to the Peace of God established by the Synod of Elne in 1027, the ages were not as dark as commonly believed, and it was the Church who carried the light, above all in the hands of her saints."

John P. Joy
Senior theologian to Most Rev. Donald Hying, bishop of Madison

"Read this book to gain a greater awareness of the pivotal role the Catholic Church played in spiritually bridging the challenging yet eternally productive span of time between the fall of Rome and the intellectually enriching Middle Ages. Then share it with your students. After all, it was during this key stretch of human history that heroically sanctifying figures oriented our gaze ever heavenward."

Justin McClain
Catholic author and teacher

The CHURCH *and the* DARK AGES

(430–1027)

St. Benedict, Charlemagne,
and the Rise of Christendom

PHILLIP CAMPBELL

Series Editor, Mike Aquilina

AVE MARIA PRESS AVE Notre Dame, Indiana

≡ RECLAIMING CATHOLIC HISTORY ≡

The history of the Catholic Church is often clouded by myth, misinformation, and missing pieces. Today there is a renewed interest in recovering the true history of the Church, correcting the record in the wake of centuries of half-truths and noble lies. Books in the Reclaiming Catholic History series, edited by Mike Aquilina and written by leading authors and historians, bring Church history to life, debunking the myths one era at a time.

The Early Church
The Church and the Roman Empire
The Church and the Dark Ages
The Church and the Middle Ages
The Church and the Age of Reformations
The Church and the Age of Enlightenment
The Church and the Modern Era

Scripture quotations are from the *Revised Standard Version of the Bible—Second Catholic Edition (Ignatius Edition)*, copyright © 2006 National Council of the Churches of Christ in the United States of America. Used by permission. All rights reserved.

Series introduction © 2019 by Mike Aquilina

Founded in 1865, Ave Maria Press is a ministry of the United States Province of Holy Cross.

www.avemariapress.com

Paperback: ISBN-13 978-1-64680-035-3

E-book: ISBN-13 978-1-64680-036-0

Cover images © Getty Images.

Cover and text design by Andy Wagoner.

Printed and bound in the United States of America.

Library of Congress Cataloging-in-Publication Data is available.

Contents

Reclaiming Catholic History: Series Introduction — ix

Chronology of *The Church and the Dark Ages (430–1027)* — xiii

Map — xvi

Introduction: Anything but "Dark" — xix

Chapter 1: Our Roman Heritage — 1
  Up Close and Personal: St. Augustine of Hippo — 2
  You Be the Judge: Did Christianity cause the — 9
    collapse of the Roman Empire?

Chapter 2: The Church among Gauls and Goths — 11
  Up Close and Personal: The Cloak of St. Martin — 14
  You Be the Judge: Did St. Augustine invent the — 18
    doctrine of original sin?

Chapter 3: The Age of St. Benedict — 29
  Up Close and Personal: The *Dialogues* of St. Gregory the Great — 32
  You Be the Judge: Did Christianity cause a decline — 40
    in education and literacy in the early Middle Ages?

Chapter 4: Missionary Monks — 45
  Up Close and Personal: Sts. Cyril and Methodius — 53
  You Be the Judge: Were monks "useless"? — 57

Chapter 5: The Church of Rome — 59
  Up Close and Personal: Pope Gregory the Great — 65
    and Gregorian Chant

You Be the Judge: What *really* happened when   70
    Pope Leo the Great met Attila the Hun?

Chapter 6: East and West   73
Up Close and Personal: St. Maximus the Confessor   84
You Be the Judge: Did the Eastern churches ever   87
    affirm the primacy of Rome?

Chapter 7: The Carolingian Renaissance   89
Up Close and Personal: The Faith of Charlemagne   92
You Be the Judge: Wasn't the Church consumed   99
    with worry over the spread of Islam?

Chapter 8: Imperium and Sacerdotium   101
Up Close and Personal: King Alfred the Great   111
You Be the Judge: Do bad popes disprove papal infallibility?   115

Chapter 9: Sacramental Controversies   117
Up Close and Personal: St. Paschasius Radbertus   126
You Be the Judge: Is the dogma of the real presence   136
    of Christ in the Eucharist a late medieval invention?

Chapter 10: The Cluniac Reform   139
Up Close and Personal: St. Berno   140
You Be the Judge: Was priestly celibacy an innovation   148
    of the late Middle Ages?

Conclusion: Transformation and Continuity   151

Notes   155

Index   159

⫤ RECLAIMING CATHOLIC HISTORY ⫥
Series Introduction

"History is bunk," said the inventor Henry Ford. And he's not the only cynic to venture judgment. As long as people have been fighting wars and writing books, critics have been there to grumble because "history is what's written by the winners."

Since history has so often been corrupted by political motives, historians in recent centuries have labored to "purify" history and make it a bare science. From now on, they declared, history should record only facts, without any personal interpretation, without moralizing, and without favoring any perspective at all.

It sounds like a good idea. We all want to know the facts. The problem is that it's just not possible. We cannot record history the way we tabulate results of a laboratory experiment. Why not? Because we cannot possibly record all the factors that influence a single person's actions—his genetic makeup, the personalities of his parents, the circumstances of his upbringing, the climate in his native land, the state of the economy, the anxieties of his neighbors, the popular superstitions of his time, his chronic indigestion, the weather on a particular day, the secret longings of his heart.

For any action taken in history, there is simply too much material to record, and there is so much more we do not know and can never know. Even if we were to collect data scrupulously and voluminously, we would still need to assign it relative importance. After all, was the climate more important than his genetic makeup?

But once you begin to select certain facts and leave others out—and once you begin to emphasize some details over others—you have begun to impose your own perspective, your interpretation, and your idea of the story.

Still, there is no other way to practice history honestly. When we read, or teach, or write history, we are discerning a story line. We are saying that certain events are directly related to other events. We say that events proceed in a particular manner until they reach a particular end, and that they resolve themselves in a particular way.

Every historian has to find the principle that makes sense of those events. Some choose economics, saying that all human decisions are based on the poverty or prosperity of nations and neighborhoods, the comfort or needs of a given person or population. Other historians see history as a succession of wars and diplomatic maneuvers. But if you see history this way, you are not practicing a pure science. You are using an interpretive key that you've chosen from many possibilities, but which is no less arbitrary than the one chosen in olden days, when the victors wrote the history. If you choose wars or economics, you are admitting a certain belief: that what matters most is power, wealth, and pleasure in this world. In doing so, you must assign a lesser role, for example, to the arts, to family life, and to religion.

But if there is a God—and most people believe there is—then God's view of things should not be merely incidental or personal. God's outlook should define objectivity. God's view should provide the objective meaning of history.

So how do we get God's view of history? Who can scale the heavens to bring God down? We can't, of course. But since God chose to come down and reveal himself and his purposes to us, we might be able to find what the Greek historians and philosophers despaired of ever finding—that is, the basis for a universal history.

The pagans knew that they could not have a science without universal principles. But universal principles were elusive because no one could transcend his own culture—and no one dared to question the rightness of the regime.

Not until the Bible do we encounter histories written by historical losers. God's people were regularly defeated, enslaved, oppressed, occupied, and exiled. Yet they told their story honestly, because they held themselves—and their historians—to a higher judgment, higher even than the king or the forces of the market. They looked at history in terms of God's judgment, blessings, curses, and mercy. This became their principle of selection and interpretation of events. It didn't matter so much whether the story flattered the king or the victorious armies.

The Bible's human authors saw history in terms of covenant. In the ancient world, a covenant was the sacred and legal way that people created a family bond. Marriage was a covenant, and adoption was a covenant. And God's relationship with his people was always based on a covenant.

God's plan for the kingdom of heaven uses the kingdoms of earth. And these kingdoms are engaged by God and evangelized for his purpose. Providence harnesses the road system and the political system of the Roman Empire, and puts it all to use to advance the Gospel. Yet Rome, too, came in for divine judgment. If God did not spare the holy city of Jerusalem, then neither would Rome be exempted.

And so the pattern continued through all the subsequent thousands of years—through the rise and fall of the Byzantine Empire, the European empires, and into the new world order that exists for our own fleeting moment.

There's a danger, of course, in trying to discern God's perspective. We run the risk of moralizing, presuming too much, or playing the prophet. There's always a danger, too, of identifying God with one "side" or another in a given war or rivalry. Christian history, at its best, transcends these problems. We can recognize that even when pagan Persia was the most vehement enemy of Christian Byzantium, the tiny Christian minority in Persia was practicing the most pure and refined Christianity the world has seen. When God uses imperial structures to advance the Gospel, the imperial structures have no monopoly on God.

It takes a subtle, discerning, and modest hand to write truly Christian history. In studying world events, a Christian historian must strive to see God's fatherly plan for the whole human race and how it has unfolded since the first Pentecost.

Christian history tells the story not of an empire, nor of a culture, but of a family. And it is a story, not a scientific treatise. In many languages, the connection is clear. In Spanish, Portuguese, Italian, and German, for example, the same word is used for "history" as for "story": *historia, história, storia, Geschichte*. In English we can lose sight of this and teach history as a succession of dates to be memorized and maps to be drawn. The time lines and atlases are certainly important, but they don't communicate to ordinary people why they should want to read history. Jacques Barzun complained, almost a half century ago, that history had fallen out of usefulness for ordinary people and was little read. It had fragmented into overspecialized microdisciplines, with off-putting names like "psychohistory" and "quantohistory."

The authors in this series strive to communicate history in a way that's accessible and even entertaining. They see history as true stories well told. They don't fear humor or pathos as threats to their trustworthiness. They are unabashed about their chosen perspective, but they are neither producing propaganda nor trashing tradition. The sins and errors of Christians (even Christian saints) are an important part of the grand narrative.

The Catholic Church's story is our inheritance, our legacy, our pride and joy, and our cautionary tale. We ignore the past at our peril. We cannot see the present clearly without a deep sense of Christian history.

Mike Aquilina
Reclaiming Catholic History Series Editor

Chronology of *The Church and the Dark Ages (430–1027)*

410   Barbarians sack Rome, leading St. Augustine to compose
               City of God

430   Death of St. Augustine

431   Council of Ephesus condemns the heresy of Nestorianism;
               Pope Celestine I sends St. Palladius to Ireland

433–493   Traditional dates of St. Patrick's mission in Ireland

440–461   Pontificate of Pope St. Leo the Great

451   Council of Chalcedon affirms Christ is one person with
               two natures, human and divine

452   Meeting of Pope Leo and Attila the Hun

476   Last Western Roman emperor deposed; Western Roman
               Empire ends

480–547   Life of St. Benedict of Nursia

484–519   Acacian Schism

496   Conversion of Clovis, king of the Franks

500 (?)   St. Brigid founds the convent of Kildare

519   Formulary of Pope Hormisdas ends the Acacian Schism

529   Second Council of Orange condemns Pelagianism

549   Fifth Council of Orleans allows kings to choose bishops
               in France

551   Second Council of Constantinople condemns the Three
               Chapters

585   Martyrdom of St. Hermenegild in Seville

587   Reccared I of Hispania renounces Arianism and converts
               to Catholicism

589   Spain becomes Catholic after nobles convert en masse

590–604   Pontificate of St. Gregory the Great

597   Death of St. Columba; St. Augustine of Canterbury arrives
               in Kent

655   Conversion of King Paeda of Mercia

664   The Synod of Whitby decides England will use the Roman
               date for Easter

717–741   Reign of Leo III the Isaurian; origin of Byzantine iconoclasm

723   The pope sends St. Boniface into Germany to preach and
               found churches

751   Pepin the Short becomes king of the Franks after deposing
               the last Merovingian monarch

754   Martyrdom of St. Boniface; Pope Stephen crowns Pepin
               in Paris

768–814   Reign of Charlemagne

773–821   Ministry of St. Benedict of Aniane

787   Second Council of Nicaea condemns iconoclasm as a
               heresy

800   Pope Leo III crowns Charlemagne "emperor of the Romans"

843   Final defeat of the iconoclasts in Constantinople; Treaty
               of Verdun splits up the Carolingian Empire

844	St. Paschasius writes *De Corpore et Sanguine Domine*
863–867	Photian Schism
871–899	Reign of King Alfred the Great
885	Vikings attack Paris
897	The Cadaver Synod
904–964	*Saeculum obscurum* of the papacy
910	Cluny is founded by William the Pious
911	Treaty between Rollo and Charles the Simple creates the Norman duchy of Normandy
927	St. Odo assumes the abbacy of Cluny
962	Pope John XII crowns Otto I Holy Roman Emperor
975	The Peace of God
1027	The Truce of God is established throughout Europe
1050	Berengar's teaching on the Eucharist divides the Church
1066	Norman conquest of England
1073	Election of Hildebrand as Pope Gregory VII
1080	Berengar of Tours is reconciled with the Church and retires to a life of asceticism and solitude

MAZOVIA

LITHUANIA

POLAND

HUNGARY

RUSSIAN PRINCIPALITIES

WALLACHIA

SERBIA

BULGARIA

BLACK SEA

BYZANTINE EMPIRE

Constantinople

SMALL TURKIC STATES

ILKHANATE EMPIRE

Athens

CRETE

CYPRUS

Antioch

Damascus

MEDITERRANEAN SEA

Jerusalem

Alexandria

MAMELUKE EMPIRE

Cairo

Anything but "Dark"

This book is about the period of European history, roughly from the death of St. Augustine in 430 to the Peace of God in the year 1027, commonly known as the Dark Ages. Merely by making this statement, we have already opened up a can of worms. What do we mean by "Dark Ages"? Dark in comparison to what? Dark according to whom? If these ages were dark, was this a bad thing? If so, from whose point of view? And by what criteria are we judging whether such-and-such era was good or bad, light or dark?

As you can see, our relatively simple introductory sentence is already giving us a bit of trouble. We'd better stop and sort some of this out before we move on.

The questions we raised pertain not to the study of history properly but to another related discipline called *historiography*. What is historiography? While the discipline of history studies the people and events of the past, historiography studies how historians have perceived these people and events. History concerns itself with historical data, while historiography is more concerned with how historians themselves have tended to view or interpret this data. Thus we could say historiography is the history of history—a way of stepping back and reflecting on the methods and preconceptions we bring to the table when we study history.

For example, to ask what sort of impact the Spanish conquistadors had on the Native American tribes they encountered is to ask a historical question. To ask why the Spaniards are often portrayed as villainous in English-language literature and film is to ask a historiographical question.

Now we are asking not about history (What happened?) but rather about historiography (What do we *think* about what happened?)

When people refer to the "Dark Ages," they are making a value judgment about a historical epoch, whether they know it or not. As we may gather from the use of the word *dark*, that judgment is negative. Why is this?

The centuries of the Dark Ages are sandwiched between the late classical era—characterized by the decline and fall of the Roman Empire—and the High Middle Ages and Renaissance, which succeeded them. The idea of this time as a period of darkness goes back to the early Renaissance writer Petrarch (1304–1374). Petrarch was a talented scholar of Greek and Latin who had great admiration for the achievements of the Greeks and the Romans. Compared to the high culture of ancient Greece and Rome, Petrarch viewed the Christian Middle Ages with disdain—as a time of barbarism in society, impoverished literature, and ignorance among men. According to Petrarch, those unfortunate enough to be born after the fall of Rome lived in an age "surrounded by darkness and gloom."

Petrarch spent the better part of his literary career translating and republishing classical Latin and Greek texts. He hoped that his own age would be followed by a brighter time, a time when mankind would enter into a fuller knowledge of himself and the world. In his work *Africa*, Petrarch wrote, "My fate is to live among varied and confusing storms. But for you perhaps, if as I hope and wish you will live long after me, there will follow a better age. This sleep of forgetfulness will not last forever. When the darkness has been dispersed, our descendants can come again in the former pure radiance." Later writers of the Renaissance would take up Petrarch's theme of the light of secular learning banishing the darkness of ignorance.

The outbreak of the Protestant revolution in 1517 only made this anti-medieval prejudice worse. For Martin Luther's rejection of Catholic authority to have legitimacy, he had to argue that the truth of the Gospel had been obscured by centuries of Catholic hegemony—in other words, that the pure light of the apostolic age had been snuffed out by the darkness of Catholic ignorance and oppression during the Middle Ages. Luther compared the Middle Ages to the Babylonian captivity of the Old Testament; just as the Jews were captive in Babylon, so the Catholic Church held the Gospel captive. Again, the age of Catholic Christianity was an age of dark ignorance, or so said Luther and the Protestants.

The term *Dark Ages* ironically came from the pen of a great defender of the Middle Ages, the Catholic Reformation-era historian Caesar Cardinal Baronius. To counter Protestant claims, Baronius wanted to write a history of the Catholic Church that emphasized the harmony and beauty of the medieval world. And thus he composed his magnum opus, the *Annales Ecclesiastici*. First published in 1588, this encyclopedic work covered the history of the first twelve centuries of Christianity. In it, Baronius referred to the tenth and eleventh centuries as a *saeculum obscurum* ("dark age") because there were relatively few written sources about this period compared to earlier centuries.

Though Baronius meant the phrase as a neutral term referring only to the scarcity of written records—and only of two centuries—the term caught on and took on a meaning beyond what he intended. The "dark ages" became the de facto designation of the Middle Ages during the Enlightenment. In the seventeenth and eighteenth centuries, rationalist thinkers of the Enlightenment believed religion to be completely antithetical to reason. The "light" of pure reason was contrasted with the "darkness" of religion and superstition. And hence the entire epoch of Christendom came to be designated as the Dark Ages.

Not only was the age of Christianity considered dark, but also the writers of the Enlightenment asserted that it was the Church that made it so dark. In a letter to King Frederick II of Prussia, the popular French writer Voltaire (1694–1778) wrote that Christianity "is assuredly the most ridiculous, the most absurd and the most bloody religion which has ever infected this world. Your Majesty will do the human race an eternal service by extirpating this infamous superstition." Not long after, historian Edward Gibbon, in his monumental *History of the Decline and Fall of the Roman Empire*, surmised that Christianity was at least partially responsible for the fall of Rome and onset of the Dark Ages. He wrote:

> The clergy successfully preached the doctrines of patience and pusillanimity; the active virtues of society were discouraged; and the last remains of military spirit were buried in the cloister: a large portion of public and private wealth was consecrated to the specious demands of charity and devotion; and the soldiers' pay was lavished on the useless multitudes of both sexes who could only plead the merits of abstinence and chastity. Faith, zeal, curiosity, and more earthly passions of malice and ambition, kindled the flame of theological discord; the church, and even the state, were distracted by religious factions, whose conflicts were sometimes bloody and always implacable; the attention of the emperors was diverted from camps to synods; the Roman world was oppressed by a new species of tyranny; and the persecuted sects became the secret enemies of their country.

And thus has the prejudice continued on to our own day.

Of course, the reality is far more complex than Petrarch or Voltaire gave the period credit for. While getting by was certainly no piece of cake in the early Middle Ages, there were also many truly innovative things about the period—including a few mechanical achievements that surpassed anything attained by the Romans. The culture and achievements of the early Middle Ages made it anything but dark. Nor can the Church be saddled with the blame for the decline of the classical world. In fact, most of our knowledge of the classical world today only exists because the Church meticulously preserved it during the Dark Ages, as we shall see.

Furthermore, we should notice that those who designate the period as "dark" generally do so based on the premise that the specifically Catholic contributions to civilization were negative. If, however, we see in the Catholic faith the light of the Gospel of Christ that brings salvation to us and transforms cultures by the power of the Gospel, we begin to see the Middle Ages in an entirely different perspective—as an age not of dreary darkness but of dazzling splendor.

We will devote the remainder of this book to exploring the unfolding of the so-called Dark Ages and the role played by the Catholic Church during this most important epoch. We will become acquainted with some of the most important people and events of the second half of the first Christian millennium. During our journey, we will have an opportunity to evaluate many of the claims advanced against the Catholic Church during this period. Essentially, we will be looking at the period through a Catholic historiographical lens to better understand the Church's contribution to the development of Europe, and thus counterbalance the old prejudices of a so-called Dark Age brought on by faith in Christ.

Chapter 1

Our Roman Heritage

On September 4 of the year 476, the sixteen-year-old boy-emperor Romulus Augustulus stood before the notables of the Roman senate assembled at the city of Ravenna and resigned the imperial office. In its long and glorious history, few of Rome's emperors had ever given up the imperial power voluntarily, and Romulus Augustulus was no exception. His resignation was under the compulsion of the powerful barbarian chieftain Odoacer. Odoacer had killed the emperor's father—a notable general—and seized the imperial capital of Ravenna. With his father dead and the capital overrun with hostile barbarians, Romulus Augustulus had little choice. The imperial insignia were handed over to the triumphant Odoacer while Romulus Augustulus skulked away into obscurity.

Odoacer could have donned the imperial purple and proclaimed himself the new emperor. Rather than do this, however, the insignia were sent to the Eastern Roman emperor at Constantinople with the message that the West no longer had need of an emperor. Odoacer then dubbed himself "king of Italy" and began the arduous process of erecting his kingdom upon the rubble of the Western Roman Empire.

The deposition of Romulus Augustulus in 476 marks the date that historians traditionally assign to the fall of the Roman Empire—at least its western half. After 476 there were no longer any vestiges of official Roman power in western Europe. In the years leading up to 476, the Western Roman Empire had gradually been replaced by a series of independent barbarian kingdoms. These new kingdoms under their rough barbarian overlords became the seeds from which medieval Europe would grow.

1

But the full flower of the medieval world was still a long way off. Despite his grandiose plans for an Italian kingdom, Odoacer was himself deposed by another barbarian conqueror and murdered at a banquet in 493. And what of the exiled boy-emperor, Romulus Augustulus? Historians are not certain what became of him. The prevailing theory seems to be that he was allowed to retire to a spacious seaside villa outside Naples and may have even been given a generous pension by Odoacer. There, by the warm waters of the Mediterranean, he lived out the rest of his days in ease, vanishing into the sunset of history with the empire he represented.

The image of Romulus Augustulus fading out of history at his seaside villa is an apt symbol for how the Roman Empire itself vanished from history. The Roman Empire did not end with a spectacular collapse—and even though we can cut the thread of the Western Roman Empire's existence in 476, it had been in decline for many decades prior to this. The empire went out not with a bang but with a slow, long whimper.

Up Close and Personal:
ST. AUGUSTINE OF HIPPO

Perhaps the greatest figure in the Catholic Church during the collapse of Rome was St. Augustine of Hippo (354–430). Augustine was born in the Roman province of Numidia in North Africa, the son of a pagan father and a Christian mother. After a riotous youth and detours through paganism, Manichaeism, and neo-Platonism, he finally found his way to the Catholic Church with the help of St. Ambrose of Milan and the prayers of his mother, St. Monica. Augustine entered the priesthood and in 396 became bishop of the African diocese of Hippo, a position he would hold for the remainder of his life.

In St. Augustine's day, Rome was in obvious collapse. In the year 410, the barbarians under Alaric sacked the city of Rome itself—something that had not happened in eight hundred years. Christians were shaken. By 410, Rome had been a Christian empire for several generations—and yet it was falling apart. "Why would God do this to his kingdom?" Christians wondered. "Shouldn't God protect his people?"

St. Augustine's thoughtful response was his magnum opus, *The City of God.* Spanning twenty-two books and written over a period of two decades, *The City of God* addresses the fundamental question of why God permits calamities to befall his own—why bad things happen to good people. St. Augustine's answer to this dilemma is a masterful explanation of the difference between the world ("the City of Man") and the Church ("the City of God").

Augustine goes on to say that, though the Roman Empire of his day had become Christian, it would be fundamentally wrong to associate God's kingdom with any earthly dominion. Though the earth will have a multitude of political kingdoms, only the Church is God's kingdom in the truest sense. Everyone who does not belong to the Church belongs to the City of Man, which is under the dominion of the devil. But these two cities are not easily distinguishable in this life; members of the City of God and the City of Man live and work side by side. For this reason, we can't so easily identify a single kingdom—like the Christian Roman Empire—with God's own kingdom. Rather, the wheat and the tares grow together in this world, each moving toward the final moment when God will sift them.

As long as we are in the world, we cannot expect to be free of calamities and misfortune. These things happen to the good and evil alike, but Augustine says they have different outcomes. For the faithful, misfortune serves to strengthen faith; for the unbeliever, they are a kind of punishment for sin.

Augustine's arguments were timely. In 430, as he lay dying, his own city of Hippo was besieged by the barbarian Vandals.

It would fall to them even as the great African bishop departed this life. St. Augustine's *City of God* reminds us that, no matter how positively we may view our own country, no place on this earth is God's kingdom. The Church is the true City of God, and our citizenship is in heaven (Phil 3:20).

Rise of the Church

Yet though one institution was coming to an end, another was about to blossom forth into full bloom. We are speaking, of course, of the Catholic Church. The Catholic Church had grown up side by side with the Roman Empire. The earthly life of the Son of God coincided with the rule of the first two Roman emperors while the Church he founded made its earliest converts during the long period of Roman peace—the Pax Romana—that spanned almost two centuries, from the time of the Emperor Augustus (d. AD 14) to the death of Emperor Marcus Aurelius (d. 180).

But the peace of the empire was not always the peace of the Church. Christians suffered localized persecution periodically throughout the Pax Romana, usually at the whims of some emperor or local magistrate who wanted to make an example of Christians for their obstinate refusal to worship the official gods of Rome. Persecution became more broad and systematic during the middle of the third century. Alarmed by the growth of the new sect, the Emperor Decius (249–251) brought the entire apparatus of the Roman state grinding down upon the Church in an effort to stomp it out. Further persecutions would follow, culminating in the so-called Great Persecution of the emperor Diocletian, which lasted from 303 to 313.

The Great Persecution turned out to be the last gasp of Roman paganism, however, for the year 313 brought the newly converted Constantine to power in Rome. Constantine issued the famous Edict of Milan, ending the

Great Persecution and legalizing Christianity. From 313 onward the Catholic Church would only grow, so much so that in 380 the emperor Theodosius declared Christianity the official religion of the Roman Empire—and not just any sort of Christianity but "that religion which was delivered to the Romans by the divine Apostle Peter"[1]; in other words, the faith professed by the successors of St. Peter in the Church of Rome.

Despite the conversion of the Roman Empire, circumstances in the West had deteriorated beyond the point of being able to preserve its existence—and Rome continued to decline until that fateful day in 476 when Odoacer sent Romulus Augustulus packing.

By the late fifth century, the Catholic Church was undoubtedly the biggest, best organized, and most influential institution in Europe.

While western Europe was disintegrating, the Church was alive with activity. Besides the continued spread of the Christian faith among the pagans of the countryside, the bishops of the Church were energetically bringing greater clarity and order to the Church's theology and governance.

Two Councils

Two ecumenical councils of the fifth century brought finality to long-standing arguments about the nature of Jesus Christ. The Council of Ephesus, held in 431 in the eastern city of the same name, was summoned in response to the heresy of Nestorianism. Nestorius of Antioch, the archbishop of Constantinople at the time, had objected to calling Mary "Mother of God." This in turn led him to deny the important unity between the divine and human natures of Christ. The Council of Ephesus delivered a stinging rebuke to Nestorius and his followers, declaring that Mary was indeed the Mother of God and that the person of Christ was a true and full union between his divine and human natures.

The second ecumenical council of the fifth century—the 451 Council of Chalcedon—addressed the heresy of the Monophysites. The Monophysites argued the opposite of Nestorius: whereas Nestorius had denied the real union between the human and divine natures of Christ, the Monophysites said this union was so complete that the human nature of Christ was dissolved into his divine nature. The image the Monophysites preferred for explaining this was the way a single drop of water is dissolved into the ocean; just so, they proposed, Christ's humanity was completely absorbed by his divinity. Against this heresy the Council of Chalcedon proclaimed that Christ was fully God and fully man, an irrevocable union of divine and human that has come to be known as the Hypostatic Union. The Council of Chalcedon was extremely controversial—the Monophysites of Antioch and Alexandria went into schism over it—but it was instrumental in settling the Christological controversies that had troubled the Church for more than a century. Though debates about the nature of Christ would continue in the East into the seventh century, Chalcedon put an end to them in the West.

Besides Ephesus and Chalcedon, a series of local councils throughout the fourth and fifth centuries finished the important work of definitively establishing the biblical canon. The Council of Rome, held in 382 during the papacy of Pope St. Damasus, formally codified the canon of the New Testament; further councils at Carthage in 393 and 419 reaffirmed this decree. These councils were not, however, promulgating a new teaching but rather affirming what had been the consensus of the Church for many years. After these important councils, there was unanimity throughout the Church regarding which books belonged in the New Testament.

The Papacy

We must also mention the growing importance of the institution of the papacy in western Europe. While the four of the great patriarchal sees were located in the Eastern Roman Empire (Constantinople, Jerusalem, Antioch, and Alexandria), Rome was the solitary patriarchal see of the West. Founded by the apostle St. Peter and consecrated by the double martyrdoms of St. Peter and St. Paul, the Church of Rome had been venerated with a kind of preeminence from apostolic times. In the second century, St. Irenaeus of Lyon wrote, "It is a matter of necessity that every Church should agree with this Church, on account of its preeminent authority."[2] St. Cyprian of Carthage (d. 258) had called the Church of Rome "the root and matrix of the Catholic Church."[3] Thus had the successors of St. Peter always been acknowledged as the focal point of Catholic unity by virtue of Christ's promise to St. Peter: "You are Peter, and on this rock I will build my church, and the powers of death shall not prevail against it" (Mt 16:18).

But by the fifth century, the Church of Rome was growing in temporal importance as well. With the collapse of Roman government in Italy, the most educated men of the age were found not in the government but in the service of the Church. The Roman pontiffs, hallowed by their apostolic lineage from St. Peter and the prestige of presiding over the spiritual center of the Christian world, became de facto rulers of the city of Rome and lands surrounding it. When Attila the Hun invaded Italy in 452, it was not the Roman emperor but the venerable Pope St. Leo I who was sent forth to negotiate the fearsome warlord's withdrawal from the peninsula. After the formal end of the Western Roman Empire in 476, the popes would become increasingly important, not only as the spiritual heads of Christendom but also as the temporal head of central Italy.

A Living Link to Rome

It is worth mentioning that many elements of old Roman civilization were preserved within and by the Catholic Church. Foremost among these was the use of the Latin language. For centuries Latin had been the dominant language in the empire. In the West, the entire bulk of patristic commentary had been composed in Latin. Thus mastery of Latin was necessary to access the Church's rich theological and devotional corpus.

Furthermore, the precision, majesty, and aesthetic of Latin made it especially suited for use in the Church's worship, especially among the educated. This meant that even though Latin as a spoken language eventually fractured and evolved in the European romance languages (Spanish, French, Italian, and so on), Latin as a literary and liturgical language continued to be preserved within the Catholic Church. This enabled the Church to nourish a living connection with its remote past. This also gave the Church a unity that transcended the various kingdoms over which it found its members dispersed. When Catholic bishops from regions as diverse as Spain, Britain, North Africa, Italy, and Gaul assembled in Rome for a synod in 382, they were all able to deliberate in the Latin language. Thus, while Europe fragmented into various barbarian kingdoms, the Church maintained a vibrant internal unity.

Roman jurisprudence, as well, lived on in the Church's canon law. As Christianity grew during the Roman era, it became necessary for bishops to formulate principles upon which to govern the Church. The leaders of the Church often turned to the principles and terminology of Roman civil law to express the Church's canonical tradition. While the content of the Church's canon law reflects the principles of Catholic tradition, its structure, vocabulary, and procedures very strongly reflect old Roman law, the soil from which the Church's canon law sprung forth.

Finally, we should mention the fact that the literary works of Roman antiquity were preserved by Catholic monks painstakingly copying the ancient manuscripts in their monasteries. But we will have more to say about this when we address Benedictine monasticism. There are many other things we could add, but it suffices to note that all of the best elements of classical Rome were taken up and preserved within the Catholic Church and are so to this day.

YOU BE THE JUDGE:

Did Christianity cause the collapse of the Roman Empire?

Enlightenment era historian Edward Gibbon (1737–1794) famously concluded that the Christian religion was responsible for the decline of the Roman Empire. Christianity, he argued, made men weak and focused their energy too much on the world to come instead of redressing the political problems of their own day. Talented individuals went into the service of the Church instead of the empire, creating a kind of "brain drain" that deprived the empire of much needed civil servants.

While it is probably true that the Church provided a more promising career than the imperial administration in the late empire, we must not mistake the cause for the effect. If people preferred to focus their energy on the next life, if men of talent preferred the clergy to the civil administration, the question is *why?*

The truth is the political situation in the late empire was rapidly deteriorating and had been for a long time. The sheer quantity of barbarian tribes pouring over Rome's frontiers stressed the Roman military to its limit. Birthrates in Rome—long in decline—meant that it was increasingly difficult for the empire to find the bodies necessary to maintain its military without recourse to foreign mercenaries. In addition, the fact that the Roman Empire had never settled on a clear method of imperial succession meant that ruinous civil wars were a constant facet of Roman life from the late second century onward. The disruption caused by all of these calamities affected the economy as well; Roman coinage was increasingly debased into the late empire, causing inflation and debt to spiral out of control. Emperors such as

Diocletian (r. 284–305) attempted to control this by increasingly socializing the economy and expanding government bureaucracy, but these measures only made matters worse.

Given this chaos, it is not surprising that people found consolation in the Church and preferred to serve an institution that was vital and expanding rather than an empire that was in its death throes, at least in the West.

Furthermore, if Christianity truly was so detrimental to the Roman Empire, it is hard to explain how the Eastern Roman Empire—which had been Christian longer than the West—not only survived the tumults of the fourth and fifth century but also actually went on to enjoy a long and prosperous existence of almost another thousand years as the Christian Byzantine Empire.

Chapter 2

The Church among Gauls and Goths

From the time of Christ until the fall of the Western Roman Empire, Christianity in Europe was spread primarily among those whom we would consider "cultured." The inhabitants of the Roman Empire were heirs to one of the highest civilizations the human race had yet produced: the subtleties of Greek philosophy and precision of Greek science, the marvels of Roman engineering, the mathematics of Babylon and Egypt, the careful exactitude of Latin jurisprudence, and a very sophisticated religious heritage. It was among this high culture that Christianity first took root and blossomed in the centuries after Christ.

But as Rome fell, Roman civilization decayed. Increasingly, the Church found itself speaking no longer to people schooled in the high culture of Greece and Rome but rather to the rude, rusticated barbarian hordes that supplanted them. With the triumph of Constantine and Christianity, the Church had converted Roman culture. With Rome now gone, the Church found itself among alien cultures that stood in need of conversion. This challenge would bring forth new saints who brought the light of Christ into a new era.

Gaul

The story of the barbarian tribes' conversion begins in the old Roman territory of Gaul. Roman Gaul was a large region composed of five different Roman provinces. If we were to lay a map of Roman Gaul over modern

Europe, we would see that it comprised all of France, Belgium, and the Netherlands, as well as portions of Switzerland and western Germany.

Gaul was named by the Romans for its native inhabitants, the Gauls, a Celtic people who settled in the region sometime around the fifth century BC. Julius Caesar waged a series of bitter wars to subjugate Gaul for Rome. Under the Romans, Gaul was a place of relative peace. The Gauls and the Romans intermingled, forming a cultured, hardy people known as the Gallo-Romans. Christianity spread into Gaul relatively early on—although how and when and by whom are all matters of conjecture. According to tradition, seven bishops were sent to organize the Church in Gaul in the middle of the third century, among them the famous St. Denis, who would later become the patron saint of France. Christianity in Gaul grew steadily but quietly.

Gallic Christians suffered little during the Great Persecution of Emperor Diocletian. The Roman ruler of Gaul at the time, Constantius Chlorus, though a sun worshipper, was amenable to Christianity due to the influence of his wife, St. Helen. Thus the Church there continued to flourish. By the year 314, a local council at Arles recorded the existence of twenty-one different dioceses in Roman Gaul. The Church of Gaul was highly organized and governed by competent, holy bishops who fought hard for the purity of the faith. A brief sketch of some of these notable bishops will demonstrate the vitality of the Gallo-Roman Christianity.

Hilary of Poitiers

The first luminary of the Gallic Church was St. Hilary of Poitiers (310–367). St. Hilary was born of pagan parents into the Gallo-Roman nobility of Poitiers and given an excellent education in the profane literature of Greece and Rome. Study of the sacred scriptures brought him to Christ, however, and he was baptized sometime prior to 350. His reputation for holiness and common sense made him a natural candidate for bishop, and he was chosen by acclamation of the Christians of Poitiers.

St. Hilary is actually the first bishop of that diocese of whom we have any definitive knowledge. This is due to his heroic opposition to the Arian heresy, which was on the ascendancy during St. Hilary's episcopate. (You may recall that Arianism, named from Arius, a priest of Alexandria [d. 336], was the heretical belief that Jesus Christ was not of the same nature as God the Father but rather a lesser divinity, akin to an angel or demigod such as those found in Greek mythology.) St. Hilary aroused the indignation of the Gallic Arians by courageously opposing the Arian bishop Saturninus of Arles at the Council of Béziers in 356. The Arians angrily denounced him to Emperor Constantius II—an Arian sympathizer—who had St. Hilary banished to the distant province of Phrygia in Asia Minor.

The banishment proved a blessing in disguise, however, as it turned the Gallic bishop into a sort of celebrity. His opinion was sought by the Greek bishops on fine points of theology, and he even journeyed to Constantinople to oppose the Arians who had entrenched themselves there. This alarmed the city's Arians, who now begged the emperor Constantius to return St. Hilary to Gaul rather than allow him to continue preaching in Constantinople. The emperor concurred, and St. Hilary returned to his diocese in triumph in 361. The resentment of Gallic Arians had gotten him banished from Poitiers, and the resentment of Eastern Arians later saw him reinstated.

St. Hilary spent the rest of his life vigorously opposing Arianism with both his deeds and his pen. He traveled to Milan in hopes of confronting the openly Arian bishop of that city in 364, but the new emperor Valentinian was sympathetic to the Arians and compelled Hilary to return to his diocese. He spent the last few years of his life at home, venerated as a living saint by his flock. He died in peace in 367. None other than the great St. Augustine would cite Hilary as an influence on his own thought, referring to him as "the illustrious doctor of the churches,"[1] a title not made official until Pope Pius IX did so in 1851.

Up Close and Personal:

THE CLOAK OF ST. MARTIN

St. Martin of Tours is best known for giving half of his military cloak to a poor man he encountered near Amiens. The scene has been depicted countless times throughout Christian history and has passed into hagiography as the definitive identifier of the saint. The story of St. Martin's cloak is almost as interesting as the life of the saint himself.

The portion of the cloak retained by St. Martin was eventually enshrined in Marmoutier Abbey in a chapel frequented by the Merovingian kings of France. By the year 679 the cloak had become the property of the kings of France, as that year it is attested in an inventory of the royal treasury. The cloak became so identified with the French monarchy that it would be ceremoniously carried into the battles of the French kings. Oaths were sworn upon the cloak, which by the early Middle Ages had become the most hallowed relic of France. Later, Charlemagne (r. 768–814) entrusted the cloak to the monks of Saint-Denis for safe keeping.

The relic was known in Latin as the *cappa Sancti Martini*, *cappa* being a Latin word for cloak. The priest who cared for the cloak and was responsible for bearing it in battle was called the *cappellanu*. Eventually all priests who served in the military became known as *cappellani*, from which the English word *chaplain* is derived.

We get another word from the cloak of St. Martin: *chapel*. When the cloak was being moved about during the early middle ages, small, temporary churches were hastily constructed on the road to hold the relic. These were called *capella*, a word for a little cloak. Gradually these little shrines lost their association with the cloak, and from then on any small church or shrine was known as a *capella*, or "chapel" in English.

Martin of Tours

By the time of Hilary's death in 367, Poitiers in particular and southwestern Gaul in general had earned a reputation as a center of learning and scholarship that attracted the Church's brightest minds. One of these exceptional characters was St. Martin of Tours (316–397). Born shortly after the legalization of Christianity, Martin was the son of a military tribune and had traveled extensively with his father on his military campaigns. Martin himself followed his father's footsteps and entered the Roman military at a young age. Soon after this he embraced Christianity, which had been spreading among the military since the conversion of Constantine. St. Martin's devotion to the new faith was lively, and he had a pious reputation.

Soon after his conversion, Martin's legion was sent to Amiens in Gaul. It was here at Amiens that St. Martin had a mystical encounter with which he would always be associated. One day while approaching the gates of the city on horseback, Martin saw a poor beggar clad scantily and suffering from the elements. Moved with compassion, Martin cut his military cloak into two parts, giving half to the beggar. According to some versions of the story, later that night Martin had a dream in which Jesus appeared to him clothed in Martin's cloak and praised him for his charity. The part of the cloak Martin retained later became a precious relic of the French monarchy. The parting of the cloak would become the hagiographical symbol to identify St. Martin, appearing in countless paintings, statues, windows, and holy cards over the centuries.

Upon his discharge from the military, Martin made his way to Poitiers to become a disciple of the famous St. Hilary. He sought and obtained permission from Hilary to take up the life of a hermit in the wilderness outside of the city. St. Martin resided there some ten years, though he frequently left to travel the countryside of Gaul, preaching to the peasants, many of whom were still steeped in paganism.

Around 371, the bishop of Tours died, and the Christians there hoped to nab the famous hermit for their new shepherd. St. Martin, however, would have none of it. The people of Tours thus resorted to trickery: a certain man of Tours came to Martin and told him his wife was very ill and begged the hermit to come prepare her for death. Martin dutifully rose and went with the man into Tours. But no sooner had he entered the city than a mob seized him and proclaimed him bishop by acclamation. Martin saw in this the will of God and consented to receive episcopal consecration as bishop of Tours.

Though bishop of a sprawling city with many obligations, he did not let his new station alter his manner of living. He took up residence in a small cell some distance from the city, soon gathering about him a band of other hermits and founding the monastery of Marmoutier. The government of his diocese was carried with zeal tempered by prudence. St. Martin proved not only an exemplar of holy life but also a competent administrator.

Despite his episcopal duties, Martin was not insensitive to the evangelical needs of the country folk about him. He undertook many missionary travels throughout the Gallic countryside in the region of Touraine, preaching to the pagans and working miracles. The seed of faith was thus planted, and within a generation the people of Touraine would be mostly Christianized.

Martin's labors sometimes took him to the city of Trier in eastern Gaul, where the Roman emperors had established their court. He came here on several occasions to ask pardon for a condemned person or challenge imperial meddling in ecclesiastical affairs. In 380 he tried to save the heretic Priscillian from a death sentence imposed by Emperor Maximus. This he did not because he sympathized with Priscillian's heresy but because he opposed the imperial intervention in the Church's internal discipline. He succeeded in getting the emperor to agree to let the case of Priscillian be handled by the Church and returned home. Afterward, however, others persuaded Emperor Maximus to change his mind and Priscillian was subsequently beheaded in 385. Martin grieved his failure to save Priscillian for the rest of his life.

Sometime after this, St. Martin made a pilgrimage to Rome and then upon his return fell ill. He died at the monastery of Candes in Gaul in 397. According to a popular tradition, recorded in the medieval *Golden Legend* of Jacopo de Voraigne and repeated elsewhere, St. Martin's funeral in Tours was officiated by St. Ambrose of Milan, his faithful friend who bilocated in order to make himself present. Miracles began happening at Martin's intercession almost immediately after his death and continued for many years.

The roughly ninety years from the birth of St. Hilary to the death of St. Martin were transformative for the Church and for Gaul in particular. When Hilary was born, paganism still reigned supreme and the Church groaned under the rigors of Diocletian's Great Persecution; by the old age of St. Martin, Christianity had been made the official religion of the Roman Empire. The Church of Gaul was established firmly under the light of Sts. Hilary and Martin. Christianity flourished there, and for years to come Gaul was a region known for its scholars and saints. One of the first nonmartyrs to be publicly venerated, the Christians of France have always considered Martin one of their greatest saints. His monastery at Marmoutier became a center of missionary activity; none other than the great St. Patrick himself spent time there studying under Martin's auspices. Such were the eminent characters who were formed in the monastic centers of Gaul.

YOU BE THE JUDGE:

Did St. Augustine invent the doctrine of original sin?

In the Pelagian controversy of the fifth century, Gallic theologians such as St. Prosper of Aquitaine and St. Hilary of Arles were the bastions of orthodoxy against Pelagius's heresy. Pelagius had taught that humankind did not need the grace of God for salvation and that we could save themselves by their own efforts. To counter this, the Gallic theologians made heavy use of the writings of St. Augustine of Hippo, whom Prosper and Hilary both considered a mentor. Augustine—following the scriptures and the Church Fathers—argued that all people were born deprived of God's grace. This is known as original sin. Jesus did not merely give us a good example to follow; rather, his death actually merited the grace by which we are saved. This grace is conferred upon us at Baptism and maintained through the sacraments of the Church. The teaching of Pelagius was eventually condemned and the theology of Augustine affirmed by the Church.

The strong reliance the Church made on Augustine in this controversy has, however, led to the unfortunate but common assertion that St. Augustine "invented" the Catholic doctrine of original sin. Is there any merit to this?

While St. Augustine was certainly integral to the Church's formulation on original sin, he did not invent it. The teaching can be found in the scriptures, in St. Paul's epistle to the Romans. St. Paul taught:

> Therefore as sin came into the world through one man and death through sin, and so death spread to all men because all men sinned. . . . For if many died through one

man's trespass, much more have the grace of God and the free gift in the grace of that one man Jesus Christ abounded for many. . . . If, because of one man's trespass, death reigned through that one man, much more will those who receive the abundance of grace and the free gift of righteousness reign in life through the one man Jesus Christ. Then as one man's trespass led to condemnation for all men, so one man's act of righteousness leads to acquittal and life for all men. For as by one man's disobedience many were made sinners, so by one man's obedience many will be made righteous. (Rom 5:12–19)

A so-called Augustinian interpretation of these passages can be found fairly early in Church history, for example, St. Cyprian's Letter 58, written in 253, which speaks of mankind inheriting through Adam "the contagion of ancient death"[2] that must be washed away by Baptism. Aurelius of Milan condemned Pelagianism and affirmed original sin in 411, before Augustine had even entered the fray. Augustine himself cites thirteen other fathers who explicitly taught what is essentially the concept of original sin well before his own time (*Contra Julianum*, book II).

The doctrine of original sin was upheld almost universally by the Church in Augustine's own day. Two synods, one in Carthage and one in Numidia, comprising more than 126 bishops, condemned Pelagianism. Clearly, the notion of original sin was no novelty if 126 bishops were willing to come together and issue joint condemnations. Finally, in January of 417, Pope Innocent I entered the controversy and formally condemned Pelagianism and excommunicated Pelagius. Another condemnation by Pope Zosimus followed in 418. Would the bishops of Rome issue these condemnations based on a novel teaching of St. Augustine? Assuredly not. In Innocent's condemnation of Pelagius, the writings of St. Augustine were not appealed to at all; rather, the Church's practice of infant Baptism and St. Paul's letter to the Romans were cited. The popes condemned Pelagianism because they held the teaching of original sin to be apostolic, as judged both by scriptural standards and the constant practice of the Church in baptizing infants.

If we look at the manner in which the Church proceeded, with its regional synods, episcopal preaching against Pelagius, and formal condemnation of his teachings, it is clear that the Catholic doctrine of original sin was not something invented by Augustine. Was St. Augustine the most thorough expositor of the dogma up to that time? Yes. Was he called upon because of his reputation for erudition and eloquence to use his pen to explain the Catholic position? Yes. Was he fundamental in the development of the doctrine? Absolutely. Was he the first to use the term *original sin*? Possibly. Was original sin "invented" by St. Augustine, in such a way that it can be asserted that this doctrine did not exist before he defended it in writing? By no means. To assert otherwise is to misunderstand history and ignore scripture and the Fathers.

It was fortunate that the Gallic church had been established on such firm footing, because shortly after the death of St. Martin, it was plagued by the outbreak of the Pelagian heresy. The heresy was named for the British priest Pelagius (354–418), who denied the doctrine of original sin and taught that human beings were capable of attaining salvation by their own efforts. In this heresy, the death of Christ was merely instructional and provided us a good example to follow. Evil was explained not in terms of fallen human nature due to original sin but in terms of poor example, which could be rectified by proper education and effort on the part of Christians. Thus, for Pelagius, Christians "earned" their salvation in a very literal sense.

Variants of this heresy took root in southern Gaul, where it was fiercely contested for the rest of the fifth century by the Church. The most eminent opponents of the heresy were Prosper of Aquitaine and St. Hilary of Arles, the Gallic disciples of St. Augustine of Hippo. Backed by Pope Celestine, Prosper and St. Hilary argued vehemently for the necessity of God's grace and became key figures in the development of the Church's understanding of grace as well as the universal popularization of the writings of St. Augustine. Gradually, orthodoxy prevailed. Remnants of the heresy smoldered on in Gaul and Britain until the Second Council of Orange (529) affirmed the teaching of St. Augustine on grace and condemned the remnants of Pelagianism.

By then, however, great change was coming over Gaul. For many generations, a Germanic people known as the Franks had been slowly migrating into Gaul. While the old Gallo-Roman culture continued in southern Gaul, the northern regions around Tournai, Soissons, and Metz were becoming increasingly Frankish.

At the time Rome fell in the West, the Franks were the dominant power in northern Gaul. The most aggressive Frankish chieftain was Clovis, ruler of the Merovingian branch of the Franks. The Merovingians were held in an almost superstitious esteem by the pagan Franks as a sacred bloodline. They were renowned for their bravery; Clovis's grandfather Merovech had won glory fighting with the Romans against none other than Attila the Hun. They were a house well attested for daring and prowess in battle.

Clovis, (r. 481–511) was brutal and coarse—a barbarian in every sense of the word. He waged war throughout northern Gaul for years, vanquishing one opponent after another in order to bring the entire region under his dominion. Once he smashed the skull of one of his men for breaking a vase he fancied; on another occasion he induced a rival chieftain to murder his own father and then subsequently killed the chieftain, assuming control of the dominions of both father and son. He was certainly an unlikely candidate to Christianize the Franks. God, however, had other plans for him.

Clovis took to wife the Burgundian princess Clotilde, a Christian. Through the influence of Clotilde and Remigius, the bishop of Reims, Clovis became acquainted with the Christian faith. Though not a Christian himself, he showered benefits upon the Church as a sign of respect for his saintly wife and the bishop. Clotilde even prevailed upon him to baptize their firstborn son; although when the child died shortly after the ceremony, Clovis was determined that neither he nor any future offspring would go near the Holy Water of the Christians.

His lack of faith in the God of Christians was about to change dramatically, however. In 496, Clovis found himself in a desperate battle with a rival tribe, the Alemanni. With his warriors in rout and men falling all about him, Clovis desperately turned to the God of his wife. The Gallo-Roman historian Gregory of Tours wrote that Clovis cried out:

> O Jesus Christ, you who as Clotilde tells me are the son of the Living God, you who give succor to those who are in danger, and victory to those accorded who hope in Thee, I seek the glory of devotion with your assistance: If you give me victory over these enemies, and if I experience the miracles that the people committed to your name say they have had, I believe in you, and I will be baptized in your name. Indeed, I invoked my gods, and, as I am experiencing, they failed to help me, which makes me believe that they are endowed with no powers, that they do not come to the aid of those who serve. It's to you I cry now, I want to believe in you if only I may be saved from my opponents.[3]

Of course, Christians are seldom encouraged to make such bargains with God. But God heard the prayer of Clovis, and immediately, the tide of the battle turned. What seemed like defeat swiftly became victory. Clovis was true to his word; he was baptized amid great pomp at the cathedral of Reims on Christmas of that same year by St. Remigius. Thousands of Clovis's Frankish warriors joined him in embracing the Christian faith, for such was the custom among the Germanic tribes: to follow their war-chief in paying homage to whichever divinity he chose to placate as well as to follow him in battle.

Clovis's understanding of Christianity was questionable. Once, when St. Remigius was instructing him on the redemption Christ won on the Cross, Clovis indignantly said, "If I and my Franks had been there at that time I would have prevented it from happening!"[4] One can imagine both the patience and frustration of St. Remigius in attempting to explain the necessity of Christ's atoning death to the hard-headed king.

Still, Clovis was embraced by the Gallo-Roman Catholics of Gaul, who saw in him a champion of their cause. For indeed he was, since many other barbarian chieftains of the time preferred Arianism. Clovis's Catholicism gave the Catholics of Gaul a reliable defender and the pope a strong ally in Western Europe. Clovis—though still rough around the edges—was sincere in his Catholic profession. He promoted Christianity throughout his realms, patronizing the Church and facilitating local synods to deal with problems of ecclesiastical discipline and the moral life of Christians in his domains.

By the time of his death in 511, Clovis had consolidated his power over most of Gaul. The new Kingdom of the Franks—or "France," as it would eventually be known—was the first of the barbarian kingdoms of the West to embrace the Catholic faith. For this reason it has ever been known as "the Church's Eldest Daughter." It would be firstborn daughter of the Church in the West, but certainly it would not be the only daughter.

Around the same time the Franks were moving into Gaul, another Germanic people, the Goths, were spreading out through Europe from the east. The origin of the Goths is uncertain—some historians place their home on the shores of the Black Sea, others further east in the steppes of Asia. By the late third century, they had made steady inroads into the plains around the Danube in the region of Thrace. Here they were exposed to Christianity, albeit in the form of Arianism. By the late fourth century, significant swaths of the Gothic populace were Arian. They harbored bitter hostility against the Catholics and frequently plundered Catholic churches and monasteries in areas under their power.

Around this time the Goths divided into two groups: the group that settled in eastern Europe became known as the Ostrogoths, while those who continued their migration westward were known as the Visigoths. We will treat of the Ostrogoths in our next chapter. Here we are more interested in the Visigoths, for like the Franks, they would become the progenitors of a vibrant Catholic kingdom in western Europe.

The Visigoths came into western Europe in the late fourth century and were part of the barbarian confederation that sacked Rome under the warlord Alaric in 410. They continued their migration westward through southern Gaul and eventually settled in the Iberian Peninsula, in the old Roman province of Hispania. Here they set up what became known as the Visigothic Kingdom of Hispania in the middle of the fifth century.

As the Franks had done in Gaul, the Visigoths displaced the native Hispano-Roman population, which was largely Catholic. The Church in Hispania at that time was respectable and organized, and it had a reputation for discipline. The most eminent western bishop of the early fourth century had been Hosius of Cordoba, the special envoy of Pope Sylvester I at the Council of Nicaea. A series of regional synods such as those held at Elvira (305) and Toledo (400) had established the Hispanian Church on a solid ground of orthodoxy and moral rigor. Its bishops were very educated and generally men of high moral caliber who naturally formed a tightly knit coterie who were a potent force within the kingdom.

As was the case in Frankish Gaul, Visigothic Spain was rent by civil wars, intrigue, and the intermittent bloodshed that characterized the barbarian kingdoms of those days. Religious differences between Catholics and Arians made this strife more acute. In some places, the Arian Visigoths were content to leave the native Catholic clergy of the Hispano-Romans in place; in others, they attempted to remove Catholic bishops and replace them with Arians from their own ranks. Often this sort of thing was done with an aim of bolstering the political power of some Visigothic leader, and thus the Church was sometimes drawn into the dynastic squabbles of the Visigoths.

For example, in 579 Hermengild, a powerful duke governing the region around Seville, converted from Arianism to Catholicism. This was due to the influence of his Frankish wife as well as the popular bishop of Seville, St. Leander. This conversion posed a threat to Hermengild's father, Liuvigild, who regarded his son's conversion as nothing short of treason. Liuvigild attempted to counter the growing influence of the Catholic Church by the appointment of Arian bishops throughout his dominions. Hermengild and Leander ardently opposed this. Eventually the conflict erupted into a full-blown rebellion. Though Hermengild had the support of both St. Leander of Seville and Pope Gregory the Great, he was ultimately defeated and imprisoned. When Hermengild refused to receive the Eucharist from an Arian bishop, Liuvigild ordered his son beheaded in 585. Pope Gregory later called him a martyr; today, St. Hermengild is venerated on April 13 by both Catholics and Orthodox Christians.

St. Leander of Seville was exiled for his support of Hermengild. He was succeeded in his bishopric by his younger brother, St. Isidore (560–636), who would bring even greater renown to the Church of Hispania than his brother had. Immediately upon taking control of his see, St. Isidore declared himself protector of the monasteries and decreed harsh sanctions against anyone who should dare molest the monks—a warning shot to the Arians of Hispania who saw Catholic monasteries as easy plunder. He preached tirelessly against Arianism. Such was the force of his personality and preaching that many eminent Arians began renouncing their heresy and embracing the Catholic faith.

Meanwhile, Liuvigild had died after a prolonged illness. According to Gregory of Tours, he suffered greatly before his death and regarded his illness as punishment for his sins. He begged pardon for his offenses and embraced the Catholic faith, weeping in penance for seven days before finally expiring in great agony—but in union with the Church.

The new king was Reccared, another son of Liuvigild. Whereas his father had opposed the influential See of Seville, Reccared cultivated amicable relations with St. Isidore. The latter persuaded the new king that it was in his best interest—spiritually and politically—to renounce Arianism and embrace the Catholic faith. Reccared agreed, and in a solemn ceremony held in January of 587, Reccared I of Hispania formally renounced Arianism and made of profession of the Catholic faith in the presence of St. Isidore. Most of the remaining Arian nobles of the kingdom followed suit. Though it lingered on for a few more years, Reccared's conversion was the death knell for Visigothic Arianism.

A council held in Toledo in 589 helped set the direction of the new Catholic kingdom. With both St. Leander and St. Isidore presiding, Reccared's profession of faith was read aloud to thunderous applause. Then the bishops, clergy, and Visigothic nobles all publicly renounced the errors of Arianism and professed their Catholic faith. Several canons were promulgated concerning the special legal status of the clergy, relations between Christians and Jews, and the moral life of the clergy.

Thus began a new chapter in the history of Hispania. Though the Visigothic habit of fratricidal warfare would continue on as long as the kingdom endured, the unification of Hispania under the Catholic dynasty of Reccared established the foundations of what would become the medieval Kingdom of Spain.

As we have seen in this chapter, in both Gaul and Hispania the older networks of Catholic clergy under the leadership of competent bishops such as St. Hilary, St. Martin, St. Remigius, St. Leander, and St. Isidore provided a framework of spiritual leadership and administrative expertise that the new governments established under men such as Clovis and Reccared could draw upon as they attempted to consolidate their barbarian

kingdoms. The threefold union of the Catholic faith with the cultural heritage of Rome and the vigor of the Germanic peoples formed the building
blocks on which the kingdoms of medieval Christendom would emerge.

Chapter 3

The Age of St. Benedict

The middle centuries of the first millennium after the birth of Christ were a truly tumultuous time for the peoples of Europe. Mass migrations of peoples across the continent, the overturning of old political institutions, the rise of new kingdoms, and the continued spread of Christianity all gave the epoch a certain dynamism that has not been seen since. It was a time of transformation—or perhaps it is better to say, transfiguration—as the new Christian culture took everything that was best about the classical world and elevated it, orienting it toward Christ.

The forces of change during this pivotal period were not solely political. That becomes abundantly clear as we examine the life and teachings of a man whose influence on the development of the Church cannot be overstated. Indeed, not only the Church but also European civilization itself owes its course of development to St. Benedict of Nursia—a man who altered the destiny of Christian Europe neither by the sword nor by the eloquence of his tongue, by political machination, or by any other worldly power. Rather, the change he wrought came through the power of the spirit manifest in the solitude of a monastic cloister.

St. Benedict of Nursia (480–547) was one of those rare personages of history whose impact is so profound that it is difficult to imagine how things may have unfolded in their absence. As the founder of the Benedictine Order and progenitor of the monastic discipline known as the Rule of St. Benedict, he bequeathed to Western civilization the fundamental structure that Catholic spirituality would follow over the next thousand years. Religious life in the Catholic West was made after the image and likeness impressed upon it by this great saint.

Benedict's World

But before we can explore this, we must say a little bit about the world into which St. Benedict was born. We have previously discussed the coming of the Gothic peoples into Europe. We have already visited their western branch, the Visigoths, who founded the Visigothic kingdom of Hispania. The eastern branch, known as the Ostrogoths, made their way into Italy in the years after the fall of Rome. They were led by their intrepid war chief, Theodoric. When the Ostrogoths came into Italy, the peninsula was still being governed by the barbarian confederation of Odoacer, the man who had deposed the last Roman emperor of the West in 476. Odoacer and Theodoric agreed to a truce, but Theodoric soon treacherously murdered Odoacer while the two were sharing a meal together in 493.

Thereafter Theodoric became sole ruler of Italy, presiding for thirty-three years over a vast Ostrogothic kingdom that stretched from Sicily to the Alps, including parts of modern-day France, Switzerland, and Austria and stretching as far east as Serbia. He took the title *Gothorum Romanorumque rex*, "king of Goths and Romans," expressing his desire to be a source of unity for both peoples—though the belligerent Arianism of his later years greatly provoked his Catholic subjects.

In the spring of 493, while Theodoric was thrusting his sword through the clavicle of Odoacer at dinner in Ravenna, a thirteen-year-old boy was pouring over his studies in an old school in the city of Rome. This boy was Benedict, the son of a Catholic noble from the Umbrian city of Nursia (near modern Spoleto). Benedict and his family had come to Rome around the time of the Ostrogothic invasion—perhaps for the greater security the capital provided, or perhaps for the opportunities it provided for political or educational advancement; we are not certain.

While in Rome, Benedict was given a rigorous education in the classical tradition. The curriculum at the time would have included a broad survey of the Latin classics, the Bible and some of the more eminent Church Fathers, and a smattering of rhetoric, astronomy, and mathematics. It was a solid education, at least as good as one could get at the time, given the social chaos that was enveloping Italy during the Ostrogothic conquest. But as Benedict grew into a young man, he became disillusioned with the dissolute lifestyle of many of his companions. He was pious, studious, and prayerful—traits that were not well nourished in the city. So Benedict left Rome to seek a quieter existence in the countryside.

A Peaceful Life

Benedict did not initially desire to take up the life of a hermit. In fact, when he first departed Rome his desire seems to have been only to live a more peaceable country life. Thus he settled in the village of Enfide in the region of Lazio. He was accompanied by his nurse, a goodly woman who had cared for the lad since his youth and did not wish to be parted from him. It was here in Enfide that Benedict performed his first miracle. His nurse had borrowed a wooden sieve from a neighbor in order to sift wheat. The sieve was broken through negligence, and the nurse came weeping with the broken pieces to the young Benedict. What happened next is told in the *Dialogues* of Pope St. Gregory the Great, the first biographer of the St. Benedict. Gregory writes:

> The devout and religious youth Benedict, seeing his nurse so lamenting, moved with compassion, took away with him both the pieces of the sieve, and with tears fell to his prayers; and after he had done, rising up he found it so whole, that the place could not be seen where before it was broken.[1]

Gregory goes on to say that word of the miracle soon spread throughout Enfide. The sieve was kept as a memento and hung in the doorway of the village church for many years. The incident brought unwanted attention to the young man, however. We can imagine the country folk excitedly fawning over the pious young miracle worker whenever he went out and about. Benedict soon realized that he would need to leave the place, and he fled Enfide and his nurse for the wilderness of Subiaco, some five miles north.

Up Close and Personal:

THE *DIALOGUES* OF ST. GREGORY THE GREAT

Almost everything we know about the life and mission of St. Benedict comes to us through a work called the *Dialogues* written by Pope St. Gregory the Great. Pope St. Gregory was born in 540, when St. Benedict was nearing the end of his life. The future pontiff became a Benedictine monk while still young and converted his family's villa into a monastery. Living only eighty-five miles or so from Benedict's abbey at Monte Cassino, Gregory probably came into contact with many older monks who had known St. Benedict in their youth. Gregory collected their stories of St. Benedict's life and much later included them in the work that became the *Dialogues*.

The *Dialogues* themselves are comprised of four books about various Italian saints. Book II is dedicated entirely to the life of St. Benedict. The work is called the *Dialogues* because Pope Gregory chose to compose it in the literary style known as the *dialogue*, in which the lives of St. Benedict and the other saints are discussed in the form of a discussion between Pope Gregory and his deacon, Peter.

Hunger for Solitude

Overgrown with brambles and strewn with rocks, Subiaco was a wild and deserted region in the district of Umbria—a place travelers passed by on their way to elsewhere. It did have one redeeming feature, however: the great Mount of Subiaco that loomed over the region from a height of more than four thousand feet. Benedict turned off the road to examine the place and found it suitable for the solitary life. There was a spring-fed lake nearby, and the sheer face of the mount featured many caves that would be ideal for the solitary eremitic life he craved.

While exploring Subiaco, St. Benedict encountered an old monk named Romanus. Romanus had been living as a hermit atop the mount for some time and welcomed the young Benedict to take up his abode on the mountain. Benedict occupied one of the caves, which was so inaccessible that the only way he could get food was for Romanus to occasionally lower it down to him in a basket on a rope.

Thus St. Benedict spent the next three years as a hermit living in a cave of Subiaco. Here he not only grew into manhood but also matured in wisdom and piety to become truly saintly. Here in the dark recesses of Subiaco he brought the prudent order to his prayer life that would later characterize the Benedictine Rule. Here, in countless nights spent crouched in prayer in his little cell, he first conceived his masterful plan for the organization of monasteries. The heart of the Benedictine Rule was born out of the solitude of Subiaco. To this day pilgrims can still make the ascent up the slopes of Subiaco and see the cave where Benedict spent his formative years. The place is now marked with a twelfth-century abbey dedicated to Benedict's sister, St. Scholastica, but in other respects Subiaco remains as wild and inaccessible as it was in Benedict's time.

Unruly Monks

Despite his solitude, St. Benedict's presence did not go unnoticed. Passersby would occasionally catch a glimpse of him. His clothes had fallen to tatters, and his hair had grown long and unruly. Some locals speculated that it was not a man but some wild beast that haunted the slopes of Subiaco. But it soon became apparent that it was no beast but a holy man living in their midst. As rumors of the holy man of Subiaco spread, some monks made the trek up the mountain to seek out Benedict and ask him to become their abbot. Benedict reluctantly agreed, although he warned these monks that they would dislike his governance over them. The monks dismissed his concerns, however, and brought him back to their monastery.

Benedict's warning soon proved true as the monks—who had been accustomed to doing as they pleased—recoiled from the discipline and structure St. Benedict brought to the monastery. Soon they repented of making Benedict their abbot and resolved to kill him by poisoning his wine. Benedict's biographer Pope Gregory tells us that the chalice of wine miraculously shattered when St. Benedict made the Sign of the Cross over it, revealing the wicked monks' diabolical plot.

After this, Benedict decided to move on and found his own monastery. He was given some property on the summit of Monte Cassino by a sympathetic Roman noble. Monte Cassino was a grand location for a monastery. The summit of the mount already featured some ruins of previous habitation, including a defensive wall and the remains of an old temple to the pagan god Apollo, whom some of the ignorant rustics were still worshipping. Benedict removed the idols to Apollo, cleansed the place, and consecrated it as a church to none other than St. Martin of Tours. The modest abbey Benedict constructed on the site would be the Abbey of Monte Cassino, the mother house of the Benedictine Order and the most famous of all Benedictine monasteries.

Wonder-Worker

From this time, Benedict began to work miracles regularly. His biography is replete with wonders of how his prayers enabled a monk to walk on water to rescue a drowning boy, healed a monk who had been injured when a wall fell on him, or banished the devil from the monastery kitchen, and many other such miraculous occurrences.

Benedict's reputation as a wonder-worker made it even to the camps of the Ostrogoths and their king, Totila. At that time, the Ostrogoths were in the middle of a fierce war with the Byzantines for possession of Italy. Totila had heard of the monk who had the gift of prophecy and wanted to test the holy man. Rather than approach him directly, Totila vested one of his guardsmen in his own royal apparel and set him off to Benedict with the royal retinue. By this he meant to test Benedict, for if God were truly with him, Totila surmised, he would recognize the ruse.

Sure enough St. Benedict immediately perceived that the guardsman was no king. The real Totila appeared before the saint trembling and threw himself on the ground before him. Benedict raised the king up and, after admonishing him for some of his wicked deeds, told him that he would reign for nine more years and die in the tenth. And these things came to pass just as St. Benedict said they would.

For the remainder of his life, Benedict traveled about the region of Lazio, founding a total of twelve monasteries. These twelve houses of Lazio were the first places where the way of life known as the Benedictine Rule was observed. As it is impossible to understand the vision of St. Benedict without a thorough study of the rule that bears his name, let us pause to learn about the extraordinary document.

A Rule for Life

The text of the *Rule of St. Benedict* was probably written at Monte Cassino, near the end of St. Benedict's life. It clearly reflects the saint's years of experience heading various monasteries. It was most likely conceived in its general outline from his early days as a hermit on Subiaco and worked out in its particulars through Benedict's years as an abbot at the various monasteries he founded.

The *Rule* was written to address the problem of the best way to live the monastic vocation. St. Benedict begins his *Rule* by describing the different kinds of monks and the various strengths and weaknesses of their lifestyles. Some suffer from laxity, those who "indulge their own wills and succumb to the allurements of gluttony" or "still keep faith with the world, so that their tonsure marks them as liars before God." On the opposite end of the spectrum are anchorites—hermits who, through "long probation" in religious life, have achieved such a level of mortification so as "to fight single handed against the vices of the flesh and their own evil thoughts."[2]

The problem, however, was that the rigorous life of the anchorites was out of reach for most average Christians, whereas the dissolute lifestyle of the less disciplined monks was of no benefit to the soul. What was needed was a mode of life that could bring authentic holiness within the reach of the average Christian. St. Benedict believed this could be obtained through what he called a *cenobitic* lifestyle. Cenobites are defined by Benedict as "the strongest kind of monks . . . those who live in monasteries and serve under a rule and an Abbot."[3] The remainder of the *Rule* unfolds Benedict's vision of how a cenobitic monastery ought to be governed.

The Abbot

At the heart of St Benedict's Rule is the office of the abbot. Coming from Aramaic to Latin by way of Greek, *abbot* is derived from the word *abba*, which means "father"—and there is no more apt description of the abbot's role in the monastery as envisioned by St. Benedict. The abbot was to have a fatherly solicitude over the monks under his care. Not only did he have real jurisdiction over the management of the monastery, but he was also a moral leader whose personal example was supposed to serve as an exhortation to holiness. Whereas all Christians will have their conduct judged by God, Benedict says the abbot will be judged twice: once for his own conduct and once for the obedience of his disciples. The abbot thus is not merely an administrator but also a true shepherd and spiritual father to the monks under his charge. He should show "now the stern countenance of a master, now the loving affection of a father" depending on the situation, St. Benedict wrote.[4]

Because of the centrality of the abbot in a Benedictine monastery, the entire character and tone of a monastery was often determined by its abbot. Because of their tremendous influence and authority, a holy abbot could and often did spark a general reform of life in those under his charge. Similarly, a lax or worldly abbot could lead the entire monastery into complacency. The story of monasticism in the Christian West of the first millennium is very much the story of continual reform under the hands of holy abbots.

Growing in Virtue

St. Benedict goes on to provide a lengthy description of the virtues a good monk should possess. Found in the fourth chapter of the *Rule*, Benedict's list is an admirable summation of what the Christian life should look like for anyone serious about holiness. It contains reformulations of the Ten Commandments, the corporal and spiritual works of mercy, the teachings of the Beatitudes, and many precepts necessary for community life.

The most important virtue, however, is that of humility. To this virtue St. Benedict devotes an entire chapter, explaining twelve steps or "degrees" of humility like rungs on a ladder that help one ascend to heaven. Humility is the culminating virtue of Christian life because it so perfectly trains the soul to love God and establishes love as the motive for all of one's good acts. In his conclusion on humility, St. Benedict says:

> Having climbed all these steps of humility, therefore, the monk will presently come to that perfect love of God which casts out fear. And all those precepts which formerly he had not observed without fear, he will now begin to keep by reason of that love, without any effort, as though naturally and by habit. No longer will his motive be fear of hell, but rather the love of Christ, good habit and delight in the virtues which the Lord will deign to show forth by the Holy Spirit in His servant now cleansed from vice and sin.[5]

Ora et Labora

After he has established the sort of spiritual character an abbot and his monks should cultivate, St. Benedict goes on to explain how a monk's time should be divided up. This is an extremely important part of the Rule, as Benedict believed that one of the most important considerations in the pursuit of holiness was how one spent one's time. St. Benedict's philosophy has been summed up in the tidy little phrase *ora et labora*, "prayer and work." We shall now consider each in turn.

Benedict knew that it was not realistic for the average Christian to spend hours upon hours absorbed in intense contemplative prayer. St. Paul had taught "pray constantly" (1 Thes 5:17). Whereas the Desert Fathers sought to fulfill this precept by doing their best to pray continually, St.

Benedict distributed fixed prayer times throughout the day instead. By punctuating the twenty-four-hour cycle with eight fixed prayer times, each part of the day was sanctified. These eight fixed prayer times became the eight original hours of the Divine Office or Liturgy of the Hours: matins, lauds, prime, terce, sext, nones, vespers, and compline.

Each canonical hour was observed by the communal recitation of the Psalms and other prayers, such that the entire Psalter was prayed through every week, with modifications appropriate to the liturgical seasons. In this way, over the changing of seasons and the passing of years, the monk learned to fuse his prayer with the scriptures—to let the prayers of the Church become the very breath in his lungs and yearning of his heart. And therein, quietly, patiently, year after year, the monk was forged into the image of Christ under the gentle, persistent hammer of Benedict's Rule.

The time not spent in prayer was to be devoted to manual labor. The reason for this was twofold: On the one hand, St. Benedict envisioned each monastery as a self-sufficient community, and thus manual labor was necessary in order to provide for the sustenance of the monastery. Hence, clearing land, draining marshes, planting crops, raising livestock, and spinning wool into cloth were all tasks a monk of Benedict's day could expect to undertake. But on the other hand, manual labor provided a daily protection against a distracted mind, which the devil was always prompt to exploit. "Idleness is the enemy of the soul," the Rule says.[6] Thus, the regimen of work, punctuated by the canonical hours, initiated the monk into a brilliant regularity that balanced the spiritual and physical in the ascent to sanctity.

But in his pursuit of holiness, Benedict did not forget to neglect the nitty-gritty of managing a monastery. The Rule contains many practical guidelines for how order is to be kept in the community: directives for electing an abbot, for how meals are to be conducted, for when visitors arrive at the monastery, for how food and wine are to be disbursed, for discipline within the monastery, and many such particulars were all spelled out with great care in the text of the Rule.

YOU BE THE JUDGE:

Did Christianity cause a decline in education and literacy in the early Middle Ages?

One of the reasons the early Middle Ages are sometimes called the "Dark Ages" is because of the dramatic decline in literacy compared to the classical age. Outside of the Church, most people in the early medieval world were illiterate, while in ancient Greece and Rome literacy was much more widespread.

It has sometimes been said that the rise of Christianity was responsible for this literary decline. Some have suggested this is because Christianity encouraged people to focus their attention on eternal life instead of solving problems in this life (the critique of Karl Marx). Others say that religious belief inevitably leads to superstition and breeds an unscientific mindset that is inimical to education (and idea floated by modern atheists like Richard Dawkins).

What role did the Church play in the literacy decline of the early Middle Ages? In fact, the decline in literacy had little to do with the Christian faith and much more to do with decline in civil and social life. The classical world of Greece and Rome flourished on a lively civic life in a highly urbanized society. The governing of the Greek city-states or (later) the Roman imperial administration required vast numbers of literate, civic-minded individuals to exercise the machinery of government. There was a social incentive for literacy, and a man's success in public life depended in large part upon his erudition.

After the Western Roman Empire fell, however, the civic life of the West went into decline. Cities shrank throughout the early Middle Ages, and the complex imperial administration was replaced by the much less sophisticated government of barbarian kings. Society became more agrarian; power was vested in land, not political office, and agriculture became more important than rhetoric. Hence the social incentive for literacy was lost— that is, everywhere except for the Church, where the reading of the scriptures, Fathers, and liturgical texts, and recitation of the Psalms, still required a high degree of literacy. The Church thus preserved literacy in the midst of a society that no longer had much value for education at the time.

Beyond preserving literacy, the Church also handed on the literary heritage of the ancient world. One of the many forms of works to which the Benedictine monks devoted themselves was copying manuscripts. In an age before printing, the only way a written work could be circulated was for a physical, handwritten copy to be produced. This work fell to the monks, who saw their scribal work in the monastic *scriptorium* as a service to God.

Almost everything we know about the ancient world comes to us through manuscripts created in medieval monasteries. For example, the earliest surviving manuscript of Julius Caesar's *Gallic Wars* was copied in French Benedictine Abbey in the late 800s; modern editions of Livy's histories of ancient Rome all date back to copies made in the monasteries of the tenth century. Our entire knowledge of the classical world is due to the patient work of monks copying ancient manuscripts.

So did the Church contribute to the decline in literacy? It seems rather that the Church preserved not only literacy but also literature itself, through the chaotic centuries of early medieval Europe.

St. Benedict died in 547 at his beloved Monte Cassino at about sixty-three years of age. It may seem a bit odd to dwell so much on the life of one man in a book about the history of an entire epoch, especially when St. Benedict was neither the first monk nor the first to organize monks into monasteries. Yet this emphasis is not unwarranted; perhaps no individual has had so profound an impact on the development of western Christendom as St. Benedict of Nursia. In 2008, Pope Benedict XVI offered some reflections on the influence of St. Benedict, for whom he had taken his own regnal name: "With his life and work St Benedict exercised a fundamental influence on the development of European civilization and culture. . . . The Saint's work and particularly his Rule were to prove heralds of an authentic spiritual leaven which, in the course of the centuries, far beyond the boundaries of his country and time, changed the face of Europe following the fall of the political unity created by the Roman Empire, inspiring a new spiritual and cultural unity, that of the Christian faith shared by the peoples of the Continent. This is how the reality we call 'Europe' came into being."[7]

This is no exaggeration. It is precisely why Pope Paul VI named St. Benedict the patron saint of Europe in 1964. The balance intrinsic to the Benedictine Rule was the admirable manner it drew out the best in a person while dealing realistically with the weaknesses and limitations of human nature. If St. Benedict's vision was to make monastic vocations accessible for the average Christian, he was astonishingly successful. Within a generation of his death, monastic houses organized on his Rule were popping up all over Europe. Women, too, adopted the Rule to the management of convents. Benedict's own sister, St. Scholastica, founded a convent not far from Monte Cassino and became the foundress of the women's branch of Benedictine monasticism.

Within a century, the observance of St. Benedict's Rule by men and women had spread to the farthest reaches of Europe. The monks who considered Benedict their spiritual father numbered in the thousands.

This alone would be an impressive feat, but the true scope of Benedict's influence will be more clearly understood in the following chapter as we learn about some of the most eminent Benedictines of the early Middle Ages and the impact monasticism had on the life of Europe.

Chapter 4

Missionary Monks

The Catholic Church and the continent of Europe are of course two very
different things. One is the mystical Body of Christ; the other is essentially a gigantic peninsula that forms the westernmost end of the Eurasian
landmass. No two things could be more dissimilar than a religion and a
continent. And yet, for a few centuries in the first millennium AD, the
histories of the Catholic Church and the European continent converged
such that the development of one was the development of the other. This
marvelous synthesis once prompted renowned Catholic author Hilaire
Belloc to say, "The Faith is Europe. And Europe is the Faith."[1]

The contours of this development were largely outlined by the various monk-missionaries who spread throughout European pagandom in
the centuries after the fall of Rome. A great many of these monks were
members of the Benedictine order. Others—like the monks of Ireland—
came from a very different monastic tradition. Still others, like Sts. Cyril
and Methodius, came from the monastic tradition of Eastern Christianity. Still, despite these differences, the overall picture is one of missionary monks fanning out across northern and eastern Europe in the fifth
to ninth centuries, establishing not only the faith but also the seeds of a
new civilization.

When Christianity takes root in a culture, it slowly transforms the
culture from within. Beliefs and practices not compatible with Christianity wither away, while more benign cultural expressions are reinter-
preted and reoriented toward Christ. The new culture that emerges joins
the ranks of all other Christian cultures but retains its own native flair,
its own uniqueness—its own particular identity. The Church has named

45

this process "inculturation." It is nothing other than the way the Gospel slowly creates a Christian framework for society.

Ireland

There are few exemplars of inculturation better than that of Ireland. At the beginning of the Middle Ages, Ireland was considered a place on the fringes of the known world. Never part of the Roman Empire, the Irish were considered wild and savage by the cultured peoples of Europe, with whom the Irish had few contacts other than to trade and occasionally pillage the coastal villages of Britain and Gaul.

In those days, Ireland was a heavily forested island, misty, and spotted with dank bogs. There was little political unity on the island. Rather, it was ruled by several different petty kings representing various clans. The only real unity among the pagan Irish was the institution of the Druids, the religious hierarchy of Irish pagandom. The Druids were a priestly caste who served as the mediators between humankind and the gods and were the objects of deep fear and reverence by the Irish people. Nevertheless, this foreboding place would soon be known as the Island of Saints of Scholars.

The first mission to the Irish was commissioned by Pope St. Celestine I around 431. Celestine consecrated St. Palladius, a Roman deacon, as a bishop and sent him to the British Isles. Palladius's mission was twofold: to strengthen the Catholic faith in Britain against the inroads of Pelagianism and to bring the faith of Christ to the *Scoti*, the ancient Roman name for the Irish. Palladius had limited success in Ireland. He managed to found a few churches, but he was strongly opposed by the local chieftains around Leinster and compelled to give up his mission.

The next missionary to attempt the conversion of Ireland first came against his will. We speak, of course, of the great St. Patrick. Born of Christian Romano-British parentage (though some say he was Gallic and a relative of St. Martin of Tours), Patrick was kidnapped from his home at a young age by Irish slavers. He was subsequently sold to a chieftain named Milchu in present-day Antrim. Milchu set Patrick to work shepherding his flocks on the slopes of Mount Slemish. Here on the windswept slopes of Slemish, Patrick would spend six years in service. But he was not idle about the things of the soul. Rather, he spent his solitude turning to the Lord. He tells us himself in his autobiography, the *Confession*:

> I tended sheep every day, and I prayed frequently during the day. More and more the love of God increased, and my sense of awe before God. Faith grew, and my spirit was moved, so that in one day I would pray up to one hundred times, and at night perhaps the same. I even remained in the woods and on the mountain, and I would rise to pray before dawn in snow and ice and rain. I never felt the worse for it, and I never felt lazy—as I realize now, the spirit was burning in me at that time.[2]

At the end of six years Patrick was advised in a dream that it was safe to flee, and he escaped Milchu by night, taking a ship to Gaul. At some point he discerned a call to serve the Church. In his *Confession*, he tells of a dream in which a man came to him bearing letters from "the voice of the Irish." These letters said, "We beg you, holy youth, come and walk among us again." Soon afterward, Patrick returned to the continent to train for the missions.

Patrick's next few years are uncertain. He seems to have spent most of his time at Auxerre in Gaul under the mentorship of its great bishop, St. Germain. He also visited Marmoutier abbey during the last days of St. Martin. He was tonsured at Lerins and ordained a priest by St. Germain. The tonsure—or shaving of the head—was a sign of a monastic consecration. There are many theories on its origin, but medievals believed it to symbolize the crown of glory merited by those who consecrated their lives to Christ through poverty, chastity, and obedience. Anyway, Patrick apparently visited Rome and was introduced to Pope St. Celestine upon the recommendation of St. Germain.

The chronology of Patrick's life is muddled at best; the traditional date of his arrival in Ireland is 432. Alas, Patrick's own autobiography provides scant detail about his work in Ireland; much of the record of St. Patrick's deeds was passed on by oral tradition. He seems to have spent most of his time in the north, around Ulster, Munster, and Limerick. His work was truly prodigious. He founded countless churches and monasteries and consecrated more than 350 bishops. Scores of saints could be found in his episcopal retinue, such as St. MacCarthem, St. Loman, St. Mel, and many more. By the time St. Patrick died in 493, the island had been almost entirely Christianized.

Missionary Zeal

The fruit of Patrick's labors was most evident in the zeal with which the new Irish converts themselves became missionaries for the Gospel. Scarcely a generation passed after the arrival of Patrick and the Irish were departing Eire for all corners of the known world as the most determined and effective Christian missionaries of the early Middle Ages.

Consider St. Enda of Aran (d. 530). St. Enda began his career as a petty king of Ulster. Yet while he pursued war and plunder, his sisters embraced the new faith and became nuns. His eldest sister, St. Fanchea, persuaded him to abandon worldly ambition and become a priest. Enda was subsequently ordained and founded a monastery on the Inishmore, the largest of the Aran Isles in Galway Bay. The monks of Aran—who, it will be remembered, came before the establishment of the Benedictine *Rule* on the continent—lived in imitation of the Egyptian hermits of the patristic age. Christian ascetics flocked to the isles of Aran, and soon the entire archipelago was covered with monastic foundations housing thousands of monks. More than twenty saints had some association with Aran, including St. Brendan the Voyager and St. Columba, the apostle of Ireland. St. Enda lived long enough to see his isles become a pilgrimage destination and became known as the father of Irish monasticism. Missionaries trained under St. Enda went forth to all corners of Europe.

We could also mention St. Brigid (d. 521), the foundress of the first convent in Ireland. Her mother had been a convert of St. Patrick. She entered the religious life under the influence of St. Mel, one of Patrick's disciples. Around 480 she founded a monastery at Kildare with seven women under a large oak tree (*Kildare* means "under the oak"). This was the first women's religious establishment in Ireland. Brigid's sisters were known for their holiness and education, and soon Kildare became a flourishing center of religion and culture. Conleth, a renowned holy man, was invited to pastor the growing community there. Kildare would grow into a cathedral city, and the abbesses of Kildare were ever after regarded as the titular heads of all the monasteries in Ireland.

Another magnificent Irish saint was St. Columba, also known as Columcille. St. Columba began his vocation as a monk in Donegal, in northern Ireland. According to tradition, he got into a dispute with St. Finnian of Moville over the ownership of an illuminated psalter. In essence, it was the very first legal dispute involving copyright. The disagreement escalated into an armed conflict between rival clans, some supporting St. Finnian, some supporting St. Columba. Deeply saddened by the violence, Columba undertook to exile himself from Ireland in penance.

Britain

It was providential he did, for he came to the island of Iona in the Scottish Hebrides. There he founded a monastery from which he would spend years evangelizing the pagan Picts, the indigenous people of ancient Scotland, then known as Caledonia. By the time of his death in 597, substantial numbers of the Picts had been brought into the Catholic fold. Columba would become known as the apostle of Scotland. In the years to come, missionaries from Iona would be sent out to evangelize the known world.

With the Irish missions having established a foothold in Britain, it was inevitable that they should also spread southward into England. At the time, England was ruled by the pagan Anglo-Saxons, a Germanic tribe that had come to the island at the time of the fall of Rome. As time wore on, Irish monasteries began cropping up in northwestern England and the Irish missionaries worked their way deeper into Anglo-Saxon territory.

But England would not be left solely to the Irish. In the same year St. Columba died, another monk was arriving in England. This was St. Augustine—not the famed Augustine of Hippo, who had lived over a century earlier—but a Benedictine monk of the same name who had been the prior of a monastery in Rome. This Augustine was a friend of none other than Pope St. Gregory the Great (590–604). Gregory had commissioned Augustine to bring the Gospel to England after (according to tradition) seeing some English boys being sold as slaves and being moved with a desire to evangelize them.

When St. Augustine and his companions reached England in 597, they were greeted by Ethelbert, king of Kent. King Ethelbert, though pagan, was married to the Christian princess Bertha and thus had some familiarity with the Christian faith. Ethelbert and Augustine met in the open fields of the Isle of Thanet. Ethelbert insisted on meeting outdoors because his pagan priests had warned him that if he met Augustine indoors, he would be vulnerable to the monk's "magic."

Ethelbert was impressed with St. Augustine and his presentation of the Christian faith. However, he was not yet convinced enough to embrace a new religion. He told Augustine:

> Your words and promises are very fair, but as they are new to us, and of uncertain import, I cannot approve of them so far as to forsake that which I have so long followed with the whole English nation. But because you are come from far into my kingdom, and, as I conceive, are desirous to impart to us those things which you believe to be true, and most beneficial, we will not molest you, but give you favorable entertainment,

and take care to supply you with your necessary sustenance;
nor do we forbid you to preach and gain as many as you can
to your religion.[3]

Ethelbert granted Augustine a tract of land in his royal city of Canterbury. The site was home to an old church that dated back to pre-Anglo-Saxon times, one dedicated to none other than St. Martin. St. Augustine took up residence here, refurbished the church, and turned it into his episcopal residence.

The evangelization of the Anglo-Saxons of Kent proceeded swiftly, and within three years Ethelbert himself was persuaded to adopt the new faith. Ethelbert was baptized soon after at Canterbury in a baptismal font that still exists to this day.

England in those days was not a single kingdom but a series of small, independent kingdoms under various Anglo-Saxon chieftains, of which Ethelbert's Kent was only one. The penetration of Christianity into these other kingdoms proceeded steadily over the next century. Some kingdoms (such as Essex and East Anglia) adopted the faith almost immediately. Others, such as Mercia or Northumbria, took several decades.

Typically the conversion of a region was preceded by the conversion of that region's monarch. For example, the conversion of Mercia began in the year 655 with the conversion of the pagan king Paeda. This was followed by the conversion of Paeda's nobles, who in Germanic cultures usually felt obliged to follow their chieftain in his religious practice. After the conversion of the nobles, missionary monks would have been invited in to found monasteries throughout the domain. These monasteries would serve a double function of educating and converting the local peasantry as well as providing centers for educating and forming native clergy.

Distinct Monastic Traditions

As St. Augustine and his companions were Benedictines, the evangelization of England largely proceeded through the establishment of

Benedictine monasteries. But as the Benedictine missionaries worked their way north and west through Britain, they eventually passed into the Celtic regions of the island that had already been evangelized by Irish missionaries. The Benedictine missionaries had known no other form of monasticism outside the Rule of St. Benedict and found the customs of the Irish monks strange. Some of these differences were superficial—the Irish monks wore a different tonsure and their abbots fulfilled a different role in the Celtic monasteries than their Benedictine counterparts. Other differences, however, were more significant.

The most substantial difference involved how to determine the date of the celebration of Easter. Following the custom of Rome, the Benedictines and their English converts observed the Lord's Resurrection on the first Sunday after the first full moon on or after the spring equinox. The Irish, however, celebrated Easter on the first Sunday on or after the fourteenth day of the lunar month, an older form of reckoning originally used in Gaul.

Representatives of the Irish and Roman traditions gathered together at a synod in Whitby, Northumbria, in 664 to settle the matter. Mediated by King Oswiu, the monks each presented the arguments for their respective traditions. The Irish were represented by St. Colman, a renowned Irish abbot from Iona; the Benedictines, by St. Wilfrid of Ripon, an Anglo-Saxon bishop. Colman defended the Irish computation of Easter on the grounds that it was the custom of the great St. Columba. But St. Wilfrid invoked the authority of the See of Rome and the teaching of the popes. After Wilfrid had spoken, King Oswiu addressed the assembly. St. Bede the Venerable records the encounter in his *History of the English Church and People*:

> When Wilfrid had spoken thus, the king said, "Is it true, Col-
> man, that these words were spoken to Peter by our Lord?" He
> answered, "It is true, O king." Then says he, "Can you show any
> such power given to your Columba?" Colman answered, "None."
> Then added the king, "Do you both agree that these words were
> principally directed to Peter, and that the keys of heaven were

given to him by our Lord?" They both answered, "We do." Then the king concluded, "And I also say unto you, that he is the door-keeper, whom I will not contradict, but will, as far as I know and am able, in all things obey his decrees, lest, when I come to the gates of the kingdom of heaven, there should be none to open them, he being my adversary who is proved to have the keys." The king having said this, all present, both great and small, gave their assent, and renouncing the more imperfect institution, resolved to conform to that which they found to be of better.[4]

After the Synod of Whitby, the question of which custom would prevail in England was settled. St. Colman resigned his abbacy in protest and returned to Ireland.

Up Close and Personal:

STS. CYRIL AND METHODIUS

Two of the more colorful missionary monks of the early Middle Ages were Sts. Cyril and Methodius. These two Greek brothers evangelized among the Slavs of eastern Europe during the latter ninth century. The brothers are remembered for their evangelical work in Moravia, where they devised an original alphabet known as Glagolitic for the use among the Slavs. The Glagolitic alphabet was especially suited to the peculiarities of the Slavic languages and became the basis for the liturgical language known as Old Slavonic, which is still used today in the churches of those regions. The brothers faced many hardships—including the "tri-linguistic heresy," which asserted that liturgical prayer should be conducted in only Hebrew, Latin, and Greek.

As a result, the Carolingian bishops continuously contested Methodius's episcopal authority and liturgy, despite constant reaffirmation by several popes. Still, the unique character of Slavic Christianity owes its existence to Cyril and Methodius, whom Pope John Paul II called "co-patron saints of Europe."

Evangelical Influence

The evangelization of England demonstrates the important role monks played in bringing the region to Christ. Whether we consider the Irish who fanned out from Iona or those Benedictines who followed St. Augustine, the conversion of England was entirely a monkish affair from beginning to end. Monks made ideal missionaries. Their vows of poverty and chastity settled any suspicions that their motives might be avaricious. Their humble obedience to their religious superiors put to rest any concern that they were out to seize the thrones of worldly princes. Their sincerity was manifest and yielded a sympathetic ear from the kings of Anglo-Saxon pagandom.

The conversion of England also exemplifies the influence the popes could have in the evangelization of a country. St. Augustine was sent to England at the behest of Pope St. Gregory the Great. After he was established there, it was the pope who sent him his episcopal *pallium*—the ecclesiastical vestment worn by bishops. When there was a dispute over the celebration of Easter, it was an appeal to papal authority that decided the issue. The papacy would be a decisive factor in the conversion of Germany as well.

Germany

Eleven years after the Synod of Whitby, a boy named Wynfrith was born among the Anglo-Saxons of Wessex. Against his family's objections he entered the religious life and spent time at the Benedictine abbeys of Exeter and Winchester. He was ordained to the priesthood at age thirty and became a well-known Latin scholar. In 716 he was offered an abbacy but declined, preferring instead to depart England for the mission territory of Germany.

Wynfrith spent some time in Utrecht in modern-day Netherlands training under St. Willibrord, a fellow Anglo-Saxon, who was laboring among the pagan Frisians there. However, a war between the Frisians and the Franks stifled Wynfrith's efforts. Wynfrith thus decided to travel to Rome to seek the guidance of the pope. Pope Gregory II received him joyfully and commissioned Wynfrith to carry out mission work in Germany.

Germany in those days was not a single kingdom but rather more of a geographic expression. The country we now know as Germany was a smattering of princedoms under various different tribes, some Christianized, some still pagan. In southern Germany, Wynfrith found the Irish missionary St. Killian had already established many Christian communities but that the regions of Thuringia and Hesse still entangled in paganism. He made many converts there, and a fair amount of those converts would enter religious life under the Rule of St. Benedict.

In 723 Wynfrith returned to Rome to confer with the pope on the situation in Germany. Pope Gregory was very pleased with the work of Wynfrith. He therefore bestowed episcopal consecration upon Wynfrith and sent him back to organize the churches in Thuringia and Hesse. He was also given letters to present to Charles Martel, the Frankish ruler, asking for his support and protection over the Germanic missions. The last gift he received from Pope Gregory was a new name: Boniface. It is not as Wynfrith of Wessex that history remembers him but rather as St. Boniface, apostle of Germany.

The episode for which St. Boniface is most well known—the cutting down of the sacred oak of Thor—occurred upon his return. When Boniface returned to his missions in Hesse, he found that many of Hessians had reverted to heathenism. They congregated near the sacred oak tree of Thor near Frizlar, where they were accustomed to gathering in times past and making sacrifices to the Germanic thunder god. St. Boniface confronted the pagans there and reproved their superstition. Then, to demonstrate the powerlessness of Thor before the might of Jesus Christ, he took an ax and began striking the oak tree. The Hessians were mortified, imagining the god would strike Boniface down in his wrath. To their astonishment, not only did Thor fail to strike St. Boniface with lightning but also a gust of wind blew, blowing the tree over with a thunderous crash. After this momentous event, the Hessians began converting in droves.

According to tradition, St. Boniface used the wood of the sacred oak to erect a church on the site dedicated to St. Peter. He would establish his episcopal see at Fulda, in central Germany, where he had founded a Benedictine monastery that was particularly dear to him. He would not remain in Fulda long, however, as he was soon appointed archbishop of Mainz and primate of all Germany. St. Boniface would spend the remainder of his life consolidating his missionary work by travel, preaching, and the frequent convocation of diocesan synods to enforce the episcopal canons. So renowned was the apostle to the Germans that he was summoned to Soisson to crown the Carolingian king, Pepin the Short, in 751.

Despite his vast responsibilities, St. Boniface still found time to visit the monks in the various monasteries he had founded and guide them in their religious profession. He spent time every year at Fulda, training the monks there for the mission fields and spending several days in prayer and meditation. It was perhaps at one of these annual retreats that he decided to return to the labor of his youth—the conversion of the Frisians in the region of Utrecht.

In 754 St. Boniface resigned his see at Mainz and returned to the Netherlands as a humble missionary monk. He had some success, but the pagan chieftains were extremely hostile to his work. While gathering with his flock on the banks of the Dorkum River in the summer of 754, the pagan Frisians fell upon him and slew Boniface along with more than fifty of his converts. His body was later recovered by local Christians. In his hands was a copy of the gospels, slashed from the swords of his murderers. Beside him was bloodstained copy of St. Ambrose's book *On the Advantage of Death*. The body of Boniface eventually made its way back to Fulda abbey, where it remains to this day awaiting the Resurrection. The richly illustrated codex Boniface was carrying at the time of his death can be seen in Fulda, still bearing the sword marks made when Boniface held the book in front of him in an attempt to save his life.

Legacy of Evangelization

The Church was swarming with monastic and missionary activity. Beginning with St. Patrick's arrival in Ireland in the early fifth century, we have followed the development of Irish Christianity and the coming of the faith to Britain—then in turn watched the English missionary Boniface bring the faith to Germany and Frisia. There are so many more missionary monks we could talk about: St. Anskar, who brought the Gospel into Scandinavia, and the brothers Sts. Cyril and Methodius, who evangelized the Slavs and even created a new alphabet and liturgy to aid them in this endeavor—not to mention all of the great missionary monks who poured out of the Frankish kingdom during the early Carolingian period (751–840). It can truly be said that the evangelization of Europe in the early Middle Ages was almost exclusively the work of missionary monks. Indeed, during this era, "missionary" and "monk" meant essentially the same thing. What was behind Europe's conversion to Christ? The answer, as we shall see, is the influence of the See of Rome.

YOU BE THE JUDGE:
Were monks "useless"?

At the dawn of the modern era, anticlerical rulers like the French revolutionaries or Emperor Joseph II of Austria abolished monastic institutions throughout their realms on the premise that monasteries served no useful purpose to society. They were seen as institutions of idleness whose purely religious mission had never bestowed any practical benefit on the community.

Yet, if we look at the Benedictine tradition, we will at once be shocked at how many valuable contributions monasteries made to the development of Europe—and continued to make as long as they flourished. The early Benedictines cleared forests and drained marshlands, making wilderness habitable. In their efforts to make their monasteries self-sufficient, they became talented farmers and herders, developing more efficient techniques of farming and breeding new stocks of cattle. In France their wine-making gave us champagne, while their experiments with hops and malted barley gave us what we know as beer to the world.

They were also responsible for many technological advancements, such as the mechanical clock (for keeping canonical hours) and eyeglasses (for elderly monks in the scriptorium). The first human flight was made by the monk Eilmer of Malmesbury, who invented the hang glider and tested it by leaping from the tower of his abbey. Some of the great pioneers of science were monks—men like the geneticist Gregor Mendel; Basil Valentine, the Benedictine father of chemistry; René-Just Haüy, the Premonstratensian-educated Catholic priest who was the father of crystallography; or Nicolaus Copernicus himself, a Third Order Dominican. Over the centuries, the blessings conferred by the monastic orders of the West upon the world have been truly inestimable, even just considering their material and scientific contributions. They were far from "useless."

Chapter 5

The Church of Rome

It was Christ himself who designated St. Peter as the rock upon which he would build his Church and promised that his faith would never fail (Mt 16:18; Lk 22:32). Thus the early Church held St. Peter in particular reverence and held the Church of Rome in special esteem, as it had been founded by the great prince of the apostles. Hence St. Irenaeus (d. 202) wrote, "It is a matter of necessity that every Church should agree with this Church, on account of its preeminent authority."[1] Many other Church Fathers expressed similar views on the Church of Rome and regarded the bishop of Rome as a court of final appeal for ecclesiastical disputes. But as we are focusing on the Dark Ages and not the early Church, we will regrettably have to pass over the fascinating early history of the bishops of Rome.

At the beginning of the Dark Ages, the Church of Rome was governed by several extremely capable men. These popes—many of them saints— were able to bring solid spiritual leadership to the Church while skillfully navigating the chaotic political situation of the age. It is worthwhile to study the lives of some of these men and learn about how the institution of the papacy helped shape the Western Church in the early Middle Ages.

Leo the Great and the Primacy of Rome

One of the greatest popes of the age was also the first to be called "great"— Pope St. Leo I, who reigned from 440 to 461. This was a time of great crisis. The political authority of the Roman Empire had essentially evaporated in the West, being replaced by the military rule of powerful generals

59

and barbarian chieftains. Leo began his ecclesiastical career as a deacon under popes Celestine and Sixtus and won a reputation for sagacity and fortitude. When Pope Sixtus III died in 440, Leo was away on a mission in Gaul and did not realize he had been chosen as Sixtus's successor until he returned to Rome a month later.

The chaotic events surrounding Rome's fall in the West left the churches of northern Italy and Gaul in considerable disarray. Leo worked to strengthen the bonds between the Gallican bishops and the Church of Rome, using his considerable influence to bring stability to the churches of war-torn Gaul. The pope's initiative here was thwarted by the influential Gallic bishop, Hilary of Arles, who resented the pope's influence on what he considered his own ecclesiastical turf. Pope Leo convened a synod of bishops (445) who affirmed the pope's universal jurisdiction, and the dispute was finally quelled when Emperor Valentinian III issued an edict confirming the decision of the synod. Valentinian's decree of 445 is a concise formulary that excellently summarizes the way the successors of St. Peter were viewed in the fifth century:

> Inasmuch as the preeminence of the Apostolic See is assured by the merits of St. Peter, the first of the bishops, by the leading position of the city of Rome and also by the authority of the holy Synod, let not presumption strive to attempt anything contrary to the authority of that See. For the peace of the churches will only then be everywhere preserved when the whole body acknowledge its ruler. . . . In order that no disturbance, however slight, may arise among the churches, and the discipline of religion may not appear to be impaired in any case whatever, we decree, by a perpetual edict, that nothing shall be attempted by the Gallican bishops, or by those of any other province, contrary to the ancient custom, without the venerable authority of the pope of the Eternal City. But whatsoever the authority of the Apostolic See has enacted, or shall enact, let that be held as law for all.[2]

Hilary quickly reconciled with Pope Leo, and peace was restored. In fact, Hilary would go on to be venerated as a saint, and when he died in 449, Leo called him a man of blessed memory.

Barbarian Invasions and Peter's Successor

The great crisis of Leo's pontificate was Attila the Hun's invasion of the West (451–453). The fearsome Hunnic warlord had come close to conquering the western empire in 451. The following year he brought his hordes into the Italian peninsula, plundering northern Italy and pledging to carry his orgy of destruction to Rome itself. In light of this threat, Pope Leo led a delegation to meet Attila near Mantua in hopes of convincing the Huns to abandon their invasion.

Nobody knows exactly what was said at the famous meeting between Pope Leo and Attila in 452. At any rate, Leo was successful and Attila agreed to withdraw from Italy. Within the year, he was dead.

The continual disruptions of the barbarian invasions posed a serious challenge to ecclesiastical discipline throughout the West. In many places moral observance was lapsing and ecclesiastical precepts were only spottily observed. Leo energetically combatted these centrifugal tendencies with a flurry of letters and decrees aimed at restoring discipline. There are more than 171 letters extant from Pope Leo, addressing bishops from all over the Church on matters moral, liturgical, sacramental, theological, and canonical.

Perhaps his most well known letter is the one addressed to St. Flavian of Constantinople, better known as the Tome of Leo. The Tome addresses one of the great Christological controversies of the early Church: Monophysitism, the heretical belief that Christ had only a single nature. Leo's Tome explains that Christ had two natures, one human and one divine, which were combined in a single person when the Word of God became incarnate. The letter was read at the Council of Chalcedon in 451. Upon hearing it, the bishops of the council exclaimed, "This is the faith of the

fathers! This is the faith of the Apostles! So we all believe! Thus the Orthodox believe! Anathema to him who does not thus believe! Peter has spoken thus through Leo!"[3] Leo's formula of "two natures in one person" has
continued to be the standard vocabulary of explaining Christ's person-
hood to this day.

Popes and the Fall of the Empire

Whether we consider Gaul, North Africa, or Italy, one way Leo had exercised his influence in a particular region was through the appointment
of a papal vicar—a representative of the Holy See abroad who served as a
liaison between the pope and the regional episcopate. One of Leo's immediate successors, Pope St. Simplicius (468–483), took similar actions in
Spain, which was in the throes of the Visigothic conquest and divided
ecclesiastically between Arians and Catholics. The establishment of the
papal vicariate at Seville aided Simplicius in exercising papal prerogatives
in Spain and helping local bishops take a unified approach to governing
the churches there.

Pope St. Simplicius reigned during the time of the collapse of the Western Roman Empire (476). Following the extinction of Roman power in
the West, the bishops of Rome found themselves assuming many of the
secular functions that had once been carried out by imperial authorities
in central Italy. The papacy gradually assumed responsibility for keeping
roads and aqueducts maintained, collecting revenues, and defending the
populace from marauding barbarians.

Popes were increasingly required to participate in diplomatic negotiations. Following Pope Leo's example, Pope Gelasius I (492–496) represented the Catholic populace of Italy in his negotiations with Theodoric
the Great. In the following century, Pope John II (533–535) was entrusted
with the management of secular affairs in central Italy by the Ostrogothic
court at Ravenna.

During the middle of the sixth century, the Eastern Roman or Byzantine Empire briefly reconquered Italy from the Ostrogoths. The Byzantine emperors recognized the pope's important role in the governance of the region and entrusted them with special responsibilities. For example, in 554 the emperor Justinian I gave the pope responsibility for regulating weights and measures in central Italy. And when the hoary old Roman Senate finally disappeared in 603, Cassiodorus and the papal court became the sole judicial authority in central Italy, a position recognized and confirmed by the Byzantine imperial authorities.

These Italian lands under the governance of the popes would become known collectively as the Patrimony of St. Peter. The administration of these lands would be an important part of the papal office, and from them the popes would draw the annual revenues necessary to maintain the administrative machinery of their office, which grew more important with every passing year.

Gregory the Great

The most eminent pope of the early Middle Ages was undoubtedly Pope St. Gregory the Great (r. 590–604). Gregory came from a family distinguished for both its civic and its ecclesiastical rank: his father had been prefect of Rome (essentially mayor of the city). His mother, Silvia, was a Roman noblewoman who is venerated as a saint to this day by both Catholics and the Greek Orthodox. Two of his paternal aunts are also venerated as saint. To top it off, his great-great-grandfather had been Pope Felix III. Gregory's family lived in a villa on Rome's Caelian Hill, near where the Roman emperors once had their palaces. The family also owned estates in Latium and Sicily.

Despite coming from such a privileged background, Gregory was not content to ride to success on his family's coattails and was determined to make his own way. As a young man he threw himself into his studies with zeal, excelling in every subject. He was well rounded in science, literature, rhetoric, law, and music. He entered city government and at age thirty became prefect of Rome, the same office his father had held. By all accounts, his administration of the city was judicious and well received by the Romans.

Despite his political successes, however, Gregory was drawn to the religious life. When Gregory's father died, Gregory inherited the family's Caelian villa. Rather than continue in politics, Gregory left public life, took vows as a Benedictine, and converted the family villa into a monastery. He was as zealous in the spiritual life as he had been in things secular, and his monastery became renowned for its discipline and the holiness of its monks.

Gregory soon attracted the attention of Pope Pelagius II, who ordained him a deacon in hopes of using his talents to resolve the ongoing Monophysite controversy. Addressing the Monophysite heresy was a much bigger problem than Pope Pelagius or Gregory could handle on their own and would not be resolved until the following century, but the assignment did allow Gregory to display his considerable talents as a theologian, diplomat, and leader.

In 579, Pope Pelagius appointed Gregory *apocrisarius*, ambassador to the imperial court in Constantinople. This was an extremely important post. Italy at the time was nominally under Byzantine control, overseen by the Byzantine exarch in the northern city of Ravenna. Actual Byzantine control of Italy, however, was tenuous. The peninsula had been overrun by the Lombards, a Germanic tribe from beyond the Alps.

Gregory's mission at Constantinople was to plead for the Byzantine emperor to send troops to drive the Lombards out. Unfortunately, the empire was then bogged down with wars in the East and had little intention of helping Italy. Gregory left Constantinople in 585 and returned to Rome after six years of unsuccessful attempts to plead the cause of Italy before the imperial court.

His devoted service was well rewarded, however, when he was elected pope by acclamation upon Pope Pelagius's death in 590. The papal office was a mixed blessing for Gregory. While he would dutifully employ his talents in the government of the Church, Gregory privately longed for the solitude of the monastery. For his entire pontificate, he would never cease to lament the burdens that the office placed upon him.

Up Close and Personal:

POPE GREGORY THE GREAT AND GREGORIAN CHANT

Pope Gregory is always remembered for the style of chant for which he is credited. But to what degree did Pope St. Gregory create "Gregorian chant"? Chant was the common musical heritage of the Church from the earliest days of Christianity. There existed many styles of chant—for example, Mozarabic in Spain, Ambrosian in Milan, Gallic in Gaul, and Byzantine. Rome had its own rich tradition of chant as well. Pope Gregory's contribution to this tradition was to arrange what his biographer John the Deacon called the "patchwork" of extant chants into a single antiphonary. His goal was to bring uniformity to the church's musical tradition by creating a single, comprehensive body of chant that could be used anywhere in the Western Church. Thus Gregory was not so much the *creator* of Gregorian chant so much as the *compiler* of it. Even so, his work was of extreme importance, so much so that Catholic tradition has attached Gregory's name forever to that chant that for 1,400 years has been recognized as the Church's official music, "especially suited to the Roman liturgy" and worthy of "pride of place" in our worship, as the Second Vatican Council taught.[4]

A Legacy of Influence

Gregory has gone down in history as perhaps the most influential pope of the first millennium, for a variety of reasons. We have already discussed St. Gregory's support for the English mission that brought St. Augustine to the court of Ethelbert. Here we are more concerned with Gregory's administration of the papacy and how his pontificate became so formative for the Church in the centuries that followed.

When Pope Gregory ascended to the chair of St. Peter, papal influence in the various barbarian kingdoms of the West had broken down, especially when compared to Pope Leo's time. The episcopates of Gaul and Spain had little ongoing contact with the Holy See. Within Italy, the war between the Lombards and the Byzantines for control of the peninsula kept things in a state of uncertainty. Into this chaotic ecclesiastical and political situation, Gregory would give himself to tireless labor for the building up of the Church, an effort even more extraordinary given that for most of his papacy he was chronically ill with indigestion, gout, fever, and other maladies. Despite this, his biographer, Paul the Deacon, says "he never rested."[5]

Pope Gregory knew that the state of the Church was largely determined by the quality of its bishops. Shortly after his election he wrote a book called *Liber Pastoralis Curae* on the office of a bishop. This book not only exemplifies the highest ideals to which any bishop should aspire but also provides insight into the standards Gregory held himself to in his own exercise of office. It is hard to overstate the influence of this book. It instantly became a classic on the Catholic episcopate and for centuries was given as a gift to every newly ordained bishop. Thus Pope Gregory's ideals continued to shape the character of the episcopate long after his death.

Gregory was zealous in his commitment to living the example he preached. He banished all lay attendants, pages, and courtiers from the Lateran palace, which even in those early days had already begun to encrust themselves about the papal court. He established an organized system of relief for the Roman indigent, whose numbers in those days were considerable. The relief came in the form of distributions of corn that were provided from the ecclesiastical estates in Sicily and used the clerical establishments of Rome to distribute it to the people.

Gregory was also a popular homilist whose sermons on the scriptures drew vast crowds. To this pope we owe the custom of visiting certain "station" churches about Rome on appointed feast days, a tradition that is still observed. To him we also owe several liturgical developments that crystallized the Mass into the form it would remain until the twentieth century, such as the placement of the Our Father before the breaking of the host and the chanting of the Alleluia after the Gradual other than at Eastertide, to which the Roman liturgy had previously restricted it.

Church Governance

By the pontificate of Gregory the Great, the lands under direct church management had grown quite extensive. Gregory proved himself a capable administrator of the Patrimony of St. Peter. But it is not so much his skill as a landlord that interests us so much as the way Gregory used the governance of the Church lands to maintain ecclesiastical order abroad. Prior to Gregory it had been custom to farm the management of the Church lands out to laypersons called rectors. The job of the rector was to collect rents from the Church's lands and organize for their defense if they were threatened. Gregory replaced the lay lectors with clerics and broadened the scope of their mission. Instead of merely collecting rents, clerical rectors were charged with filling vacant sees, holding local synods, quashing heresy, providing for the physical maintenance of churches and monasteries, reforming abuses, enforcing ecclesiastical discipline, and even chastising local bishops in the pope's name if they were found to be acting amiss. Essentially, the rectors became a means by which Pope Gregory was able to keep abreast of affairs in far-off regions and exercise his jurisdiction effectively.

The Mother of All Churches

There is no doubt that Gregory viewed the See of Rome as the mother of all the churches, and the papal office having a primacy not just of honor but of actual jurisdiction. His surviving letters reveal his thinking clearly on the question. He intervened in other dioceses when their churches were in disarray; he commanded sees to elect new bishops if their current occupants were unworthy; he was inflexible in his insistence on fiscal responsibility and the observance of clerical celibacy; he calls the Apostolic See "the head of all churches" and says that "I, though unworthy, have been set up in command of the Church"[6]; he teaches that it is his approval that gives force to the decrees of synods and councils and that he likewise has the power to annul them; and he says that other patriarchs might make appeals to him and that he has the authority to judge and correct other bishops.

It is clear that Gregory operated under the assumption that all were subject to the jurisdiction of the See of Rome. This does not mean Gregory was an autocrat or a tyrant; indeed, he respected the autonomy and privileges of other bishops and metropolitans as much as possible. Even so, if circumstances warranted, he was not averse to using the power of the Holy See to rectify problems throughout the Church wherever they might be. And he did everything possible to preserve, strengthen, and expand the prerogatives of the papacy.

The final years of Gregory's life constituted a significant cross for him. The weight of the papal office gave him no reprieve, but his physical ailments only grew worse. He finally died on March 12, 604, at around sixty-four years of age. He was canonized swiftly after his death by universal acclamation. The influence of this pope can hardly be overstated.

The fact that sixteen pontiffs of the Catholic Church have born his name is a testament to the enduring legacy of Gregory the Great.

Primacy of Rome

Ever since the earliest days of Christianity, the Church of Rome and its bishop had been held in special esteem by Christians everywhere. Whether we look to the East or the West, we see Christians turning to the bishop of Rome to adjudicate disputes, proclaim orthodoxy, and defend the prerogatives of the Church. Hallowed by its founding by St. Peter and the martyrdoms of both Paul and Peter, early Christians revered the Church of Rome, recalling that it was upon Peter that Christ established his Church. As St. Cyprian once wrote,

> A primacy is given to Peter, whereby it is made clear that there is but one Church and one chair. . . . If someone does not hold fast to this unity of Peter, can he imagine that he still holds the faith? If he [should] desert the chair of Peter upon whom the Church was built, can he still be confident that he is in the Church?[7]

It was established as the visible source of unity among Christians by Jesus himself.

The importance of the Church of Rome only increased after the fall of Rome. The pope remained the only figure in the West with the resources and moral authority to bring order into the chaos that followed in the wake of the empire's collapse. Energetic pontiffs like Leo, Gelasius, Simplicius, John II, and Gregory worked tirelessly to maintain discipline amid the tumults of the barbarian kingdoms. Throughout the fifth, sixth, and seventh centuries, the Church of Rome developed into a highly organized bureaucracy, becoming not only the symbolic heart of Christendom but also its administrative heart. This authority had always been implicit in the Church's understanding of the Apostolic See; as early as the time of Pope

St. Clement I (88–99) we already see the pope intervening in other dioceses to restore order and acting as a court of final appeal for the Church.

The development of the papacy between the time of Leo and Gregory was nothing other than the gradual unfolding of an authority Christians had generally understood the Church of Rome to possess—save that the disorders of the early Middle Ages made the exercise of this authority more necessary. Meanwhile the disciplines of Rome—as well as its liturgy—gradually spread throughout the Latin-speaking world, bringing greater unity to the scattered dioceses of the barbarian age. That's not to say there were never disputes about the proper place of the Roman Church in the order of things. After the capital of the Roman Empire moved east to Constantinople, the patriarchs of that city would become the most persistent detractors of the pope's prerogatives. Next, we will sketch out the history of relations between the churches of the Latin-speaking West and the Greek-speaking East.

YOU BE THE JUDGE:

What really *happened when Pope Leo the Great met Attila the Hun?*

In the year 452, Pope Leo the Great and a Roman delegation went out to meet the fearsome Hunnic warlord Attila, who was then rampaging his way southward through Italy toward Rome. The purpose of the meeting was to persuade Attila to leave off his planned attack on Rome. The two great leaders met, and by the time it was over, Attila had changed his mind and turned his army around, deciding instead to spare Rome and return to his camp for the winter.

Nobody really knows what Pope Leo said at this famous meeting to dissuade Attila, but two different accounts have come down to us. The first comes from the writer Prosper of Aquitaine, who wrote in 455, only three years after the events and within the lifetime of Pope St. Leo. Prosper stated merely that "when [Attila] had received the embassy, he was so impressed by the presence of the high priest [Pope Leo] that he ordered his army to give up warfare and, after he had promised peace, he departed beyond the Danube."[8]

Some years later, in a life of Pope St. Leo written by an anonymous chronicler, we see a more detailed variant of the story. In the second version, Pope Leo humbles himself before Attila and asks for mercy for the people of Rome. The chronicle says:

> As Leo said these things Attila stood looking upon his venerable garb and aspect, silent, as if thinking deeply. And lo, suddenly there were seen the apostles Peter and Paul, clad like bishops, standing by Leo, the one on the right hand, the other on the left. They held swords stretched out over his head, and threatened Attila with death if he did not obey the pope's command. Wherefore Attila was appeased he who had raged as one mad. He by Leo's intercession, straightway promised a lasting peace and withdrew beyond the Danube.[9]

What do you think really happened? We will probably never know.

Chapter 6

East and West

Jesus Christ established his Church "in the fullness of time," as St. Paul says in Galatians 4:4. At that time Europe, North Africa, and the Middle East were united politically and culturally under the aegis of the Roman Empire during the Pax Romana ushered in by the emperor Augustus. Perhaps you have never paused to consider what exactly constitutes an *empire*, as opposed to, say, a mere kingdom. Whereas a kingdom is a single nation under the rule of a king or queen, an empire is a conglomeration of many varied nations and peoples united under an emperor. Empires use their sociopolitical might to hold together what would otherwise be a disparate cacophony of peoples and languages. The Roman world of Jesus Christ's day possessed a cultural unity that most of us living today have not experienced.

In this atmosphere it was easy for the Church to spread her message and thrive. Using the reliable system of Roman roads, a Christian missionary could start off by foot on Jerusalem and walk as far as Italy or Spain if he so wished. Though Roman law was often against the Church in the beginning, its universality ensured that the Church had a stable political environment in which to grow. Christians from far-flung corners of the empire felt great kinship with one another. When Athanasius of Alexandria, Egypt, was exiled from his see by an Arian emperor in 335, he went to the west German city of Trier, where he made a home for himself and was received with joy by the local Church. It is strange today to think that a native Egyptian would feel at home in Germany and be able to converse with his brother Christians in the same tongue, but such was the cultural unity of the Roman world. To be sure, people retained their various cultural distinctiveness—they still spoke their own native languages at home, revered their own gods, and went about in their own ethnic clothing—but all of this was within the even bigger cultural umbrella of *Romanitas*, the "Roman-ness" that bound the empire together.

Breaking Up Is Hard to Do

However, when the Roman polity began to collapse in the fourth and fifth centuries, the cultural unity the empire had enjoyed also began to fracture. In the chaotic years surrounding the fall of Rome, it became increasingly clear that the essential cultural division in this brave new world was between the Greek-speaking East and the Latin-speaking West. The removal of the imperial capital to the eastern city of Constantinople in 330 was also a catalyst for this divide. With the capital now situated in a Greek-speaking part of the empire, it was inevitable that a new Greek-speaking administrative class would emerge alongside the older Latin-speaking nobility of the West.

When Theodosius I died in 395, this division had become so pronounced that the empire was officially split into two halves. From 395 on, the West and East would only drift further apart culturally and politically. The Church was deeply affected by this estrangement.

When Christianity was legalized in 313, there were four major or "patriarchal" sees in the Church: Rome, Antioch, Jerusalem, and Alexandria. Following the founding of Constantinople in 330, however, this new imperial capital quickly grew in importance, as did its bishops. The Church of Constantinople grew in prestige under the presidency of the holy and erudite bishops St. Gregory Nazianzus and St. John Chrysostom. Constantinople found itself elevated to the level of a patriarchal see, taking its place alongside Rome, Antioch, and the others as one of the principal churches of the Christian world.

However, this newfound importance begged some important questions: Where did Constantinople rank in the hierarchy of the patriarchal sees? Did it matter that the imperial capital was now located there? What was the relationship of Constantinople to Rome?

Rome versus Constantinople

These questions would come to the fore in 381 when Pope Damasus recommended that the emperor Theodosius summon an ecumenical council to settle a dispute over the rightful successor to the see of Constantinople. This would become the Council of Constantinople, the Church's second ecumenical council. It is not necessary to rehash all the details of the council, but for our purposes the most important act of the Council of Constantinople was its Third Canon, which said, "The Bishop of Constantinople, however, shall have the prerogative of honor after the Bishop of Rome; because Constantinople is New Rome."[1]

This canon effectively demoted Antioch, Alexandria, and Jerusalem, and elevated Constantinople to the highest position possible within the hierarchy after Rome. Rome subsequently disputed the validity of this canon over the years. None other than the great Pope Leo protested that the Third Canon had never been ratified by Rome and that it unjustly downgraded the other sees. In a letter to Anatolius, bishop of Constantinople, Pope Leo wrote in the year 452:

> I grieve, beloved, that you have fallen into this too, that you should try to break down the most sacred constitutions . . . as if this opportunity had expressly offered itself to you for the See of Alexandria to lose its privilege of second place, and the church of Antioch to forego its right to being third in dignity, in order that when these places had been subjected to your jurisdiction, all metropolitan bishops might be deprived of their proper honor. . . . For your purpose is in no way whatever supported by the written assent of certain bishops given, as you

allege, sixty years ago, and never brought to the knowledge of
the Apostolic See by your predecessors.[2]

Disputes between Rome and Constantinople would continue. Sometimes the dispute was theological, brought about when a Constantinopolitan patriarch wanted to affirm some pet heresy of the reigning emperor. Other times it was a canonical dispute about who was the rightful occupant of the see of Constantinople. Still other disagreements concerned the prerogatives of the Holy See. Several of these conflicts boiled over into open schism.

Growing Schism

The first of these episodes was the Acacian Schism of 484–519. In the late fifth century, the churches of the East were rent by the Monophysite heresy, which taught that Christ had but a single nature that was wholly divine. Monophysitism had been condemned by the Council of Chalcedon in 451, as we previously discussed. Nevertheless, the heresy persisted, especially in Syria and Egypt, to the point that the unity of the Byzantine Empire was threatened.

The patriarch of Constantinople at this time was Acacius. Under the patronage of the emperor Zeno, Acacius drew up an edict called the *Henotikon* ("Edict of Union") that was meant to reconcile Chalcedonian Christians with the Monophysites. The *Henotikon* was essentially a compromise document that recognized Christ's divinity but was silent on the question of his natures.

The *Henotikon* failed to satisfy either side—Chalcedonian Christians were criticized it for not affirming Christ's human nature, while the Monophysites ridiculed it for failing to explicitly affirm their heresy. All sides castigated Emperor Zeno for meddling in theological affairs. In Rome, Pope Felix III condemned the document as intentionally vague and summoned Patriarch Acacius to Rome to answer for it. Acacius refused and was excommunicated by Felix in 484, as were those in communion with him. Acacius responded by striking Pope Felix's name from the diptychs (the official lists of those who were commemorated in the prayers of the liturgy).

The schism persisted beyond the deaths of both Felix (492) and Acacius (489). Various half-hearted attempts were made to reconcile, but it was not until a new imperial dynasty came to power under Emperor Justin I (r. 518–527) that the Byzantines made a sincere effort to remedy the schism. In 519, with the support of the new patriarch, John of Cappadocia, Justin I and Pope Hormisdas agreed to end the schism. The emperor proclaimed his adherence to the Council of Chalcedon, Acacius was condemned, and the patriarch of Constantinople professed the subordination of the See of Constantinople to the See of Rome. Thus the schism was ended.

The Three Chapters

A generation later, however, another rift emerged between the East and the West in the so-called controversy of the Three Chapters. The controversy of the Three Chapters was achingly complex, and we will not try to untangle it all here, but it suffices to say the crux of the dispute was another attempt by the Byzantine emperor—now Justinian I—to reunite Monophysites and Chalcedonians.

To this end, Justinian proposed the condemnation of a series of writings called the Three Chapters. These were a collection of writings by fifth-century theologians that were suspected of Nestorianism (the heresy that Christ was two separate persons, one human and one divine). Since both Chalcedonians and Monophysites condemned Nestorianism, Justinian hoped the condemnation of the Three Chapters would bring the two sides together.

Unfortunately, the Three Chapters also contained important affirmations of Christ's dual natures, such that condemning them would result in an effective revision of the Council of Chalcedon and a weakening of the Church's teaching on Christ's two natures. Consequently, many bishops, especially of the West, refused to condemn the Three Chapters, which led to substantial disagreement. Pope Vigilius vacillated, at first condemning the Three Chapters under imperial pressure but then withdrawing his condemnation, for which he was summoned to Constantinople and placed under house arrest. To make matters worse, most of the Western bishops by this time were unable to read Greek and thus were not capable of evaluating the texts in question for themselves.

An ecumenical council was summoned in 551 to settle the matter. The council, known as the Second Council of Constantinople, condemned the Three Chapters. Pope Vigilius, though present in Constantinople, declined to attend the council. For this, the council struck Vigilius's name from the diptychs and the emperor had him imprisoned. Vigilius reluctantly condemned the Three Chapters in 553. In response, some of the north Italian dioceses like Milan and Aquileia broke communion with Rome—and the Visigoths simply refused to acknowledge the council. By and large, however, the council was accepted without protest across the West. Milan and Aquileia were back in communion with Rome within a few decades. As for Justinian, the controversy he stirred up over the Three Chapters ended up yielding very negligible benefits. By this time, the Monophysites of the East had been persevering in their heresy for more than two hundred years, and nothing was likely to change that.

Pope Vigilius's vacillating over the condemnation of the Three Chapters is sometimes cited as an argument against papal infallibility. We should keep in mind, however, that the theological issues involved were extremely complex, and made more so by Vigilius's inability to read the texts in their original Greek. Vigilius's statements on the Three Chapters were always vague and hedged with qualifications. Furthermore, he was under duress for much of the controversy, having spent years as a virtual prisoner in Rome. If he did err in any of his official pronouncements, it was on a level far below that required to fulfill the conditions of papal infallibility. Even so, it seems the most Vigilius can be condemned for is ambiguity and temerity.

An "Ecumenical" Patriarch

A generation later, conflict again broke out between the East and the West when the new patriarch of Constantinople, John the Faster, adopted the title "ecumenical patriarch." Though patriarchs of Constantinople had sometimes been addressed as *oikoumenikos* before, Pope St. Gregory the Great was alarmed by the Latin translation of the title, "universal patriarch," which seemed to imply an authority over the other bishops. In fact, *oikoumenikos* simply meant that the bishop of Constantinople had a special role as primate of the East given Constantinople's status as imperial capital.

Even so, the title seemed presumptuous to Pope Gregory. The holy pontiff never ceased to defend the prerogatives of Rome when they were questioned. To the bishop of Syracuse, Gregory said that he knew of no bishop not ultimately subject to the Apostolic See.[3] As for the "ecumenical patriarch," he said, "For as to what they say about the Church of Constantinople, who can doubt that it is subject to the Apostolic See, as both the most pious lord the emperor and our brother the bishop of that city continually acknowledge?"[4]

During the controversy, Eulogius, patriarch of Alexandria, sent Pope Gregory an effusive letter of support, praising the authority of the chair of Peter and the pontificate of Gregory. Gregory responded with gratitude in a letter of his own: "Your most sweet Holiness has spoken much in your letter to me about the chair of Saint Peter, Prince of the apostles, saying that he himself now sits on it in the persons of his successors. And indeed I acknowledge myself to be unworthy, not only in the dignity of such as preside, but even in the number of such as stand."[5] He then follows with a concise explication of the authority of the Petrine See, grounded in the sacred scriptures:

> Who can be ignorant that holy Church has been made firm in the solidity of the Prince of the apostles, who derived his name from the firmness of his mind, so as to be called Petrus from *petra*. And to him it is said by the voice of the Truth, "To you I will give the keys of the kingdom of heaven." And again it is said to him, "And when you are converted, strengthen your brethren." And once more, "Simon, son of Jonas, do you love Me? Feed my sheep." Wherefore though there are many apostles, yet with regard to the principality itself the See of the Prince of the apostles alone has grown strong in authority.[6]

When John refused to give up the title, Gregory subsequently forbid his legate in Constantinople from receiving Holy Communion together with John. John responded by accusing one of Gregory's presbyters of heresy, and the controversy degenerated into a petty squabble. In the end, John kept the title, which has been used by the patriarchs of Constantinople to this day. All Gregory could do was imitate his rival by creating a new title for himself: *servus servorum Dei*, that is, "servant of the servants of God." Gregory thus hoped by this humble title to offer a wholesome counterexample to what he perceived as the hubris of Patriarch John. *Servus servorum Dei* is likewise a title that has been retained by the popes to this day.

Icons and Iconoclasm

Perhaps the most severe schism between East and West during the first millennium was during the iconoclast era. Iconoclasm was a heresy that denied the validity of including images in Christian worship. Since the earliest days of Christianity, Christians had used images in their liturgies. The earliest images can be found on the catacombs of Rome, decorating the walls and ceilings of ancient chapels where commemorative Masses were said over the tombs of the martyrs. After the age of persecution, the proliferation of Christian churches saw the widespread adoption of images as decorative and liturgical elements. By the early eighth century, a certain stylized two-dimensional representation of Christ and the saints commonly known as *icons* had become normative in the churches of the East.

The dispute over icons began not with any cleric but with the Byzantine emperor Leo III the Isaurian (r. 717–741), who began a campaign to rid Byzantium of icons in 726. His motivations are unclear. Some say it was an attempt to strike at the power of the monasteries, which were exceptionally influential politically in the East and were avid promoters of icons. Others say there was a legitimate concern that liturgical use of icons was devolving into superstition. Still others note that Emperor Leo was raised on the empire's eastern frontiers and may have been influenced by Islamic theology.

At any rate, imperial troops were marshaled throughout the empire to destroy or whitewash icons. This was very unpopular with the populace and was vociferously opposed by the monks. The patriarch of Constantinople resigned rather than enforce the emperor's edict. The reigning pontiff, Pope St. Gregory III, upon hearing of these actions, summoned two synods that condemned the actions of Emperor Leo. In response Leo confiscated papal estates in Calabria and Sicily, as well as removing the province of Illyricum from papal governance and placing them all under the governance of the newly appointed patriarchate of Constantinople. This was pivotal, as these regions contained the only Greek-speaking Christians still under the pope's jurisdiction. Essentially, this act took the jurisdictional disputes between East and West and formalized them geographically.

Iconoclasm continued under Emperor Leo's son, Constantine V Copronymous, a cognomen that means "Name of Dung." He summoned a regional council at Heira in 754 and condemned the veneration of icons. The pope was neither invited nor represented, and all of the bishops in attendance were personally selected by Constantine. A general persecution of monasteries and iconophiles followed, including the killing of prominent monks who were too vocal in their opposition to the emperor.

After Constantine's death in 775, power eventually devolved to his daughter-in-law, the empress Irene. Irene was an iconophile who sought reconciliation with the West and the restoration of icons, not only for religious reasons but also to help cement her tenuous grasp on power. Accordingly, she summoned the Second Council of Nicaea in 787, where the Church worked out its beautiful teaching on the veneration of images. With bishops of the East and West participating (Pope Adrian I being represented by his legates), the council affirmed the practice of venerating images. A letter of the pope was read approving the veneration of images. When the bishops heard Pope Adrian's words, they cried out, "We follow! We receive! We admit!" Finally the following declaration was issued at the close of the council:

> As the sacred and life-giving cross is everywhere set up as a symbol, so also should the images of Jesus Christ, the Virgin Mary, the holy angels, as well as those of the saints and other pious and holy men be embodied in the manufacture of sacred vessels, tapestries, vestments, etc., and exhibited on the walls of churches, in the homes, and in all conspicuous places, by the roadside and everywhere, to be revered by all who might see them. For the more they are contemplated, the more they move to fervent memory of their prototypes.

> Therefore, it is proper to accord to them a fervent and reverent veneration, not, however, the veritable adoration which, according to our faith, belongs to the Divine Being alone—for the honor accorded to the image passes over to its prototype, and whoever venerate the image venerate in it the reality of what is there represented.[7]

Iconoclasm still had one last gasp, however. Despite the success of the council, Irene was deposed by a military coup in 802. Iconoclasm had been popular with the army and would undergo a brief revival under Leo V. Second Nicaea was repudiated, the Council of Hiera was reaffirmed, and once again icons were whitewashed throughout the East. However, Leo V was assassinated in 820. Future emperors dallied with the heresy for a time, but its heyday had passed. Icons were formally subsequently restored with great celebration in 843. Since then, the first Sunday of Lent for Eastern Christians has been observed as the Feast of the Restoration of Orthodoxy.

This marked the end of the iconoclast era and the restoration of full communion with the West. By this time, however, the popes had grown weary of perceived Byzantine duplicity, religious teeter-tottering, and political instability. The relationship with Byzantium was often fraught with tension and yielded them little tangible benefits in the way of military assistance against the Lombards in Italy. Beginning in the mid-eighth century, the popes turned westward, valuing their relationship with the Frankish kingdom of the Carolingians above that with Constantinople. The West and East were continuing their long drift apart.

Up Close and Personal:

ST. MAXIMUS THE CONFESSOR

During the Christological controversies of the seventh century, one of the most eminent theologians was the Byzantine monk St. Maximus the Confessor. Against the Monothelitist heresy (which taught that Christ had two natures but only a single "theandric" or divine-human will), St. Maximus espoused the orthodox position that Jesus had a human will and a divine will, corresponding to his two natures.

After converting a notable Monothelitist heretic in Carthage, St. Maximus traveled to Rome and with Pope Martin I took part in the Lateran Council of 649, which formally condemned the heresy. This angered the Byzantine emperor Constans II, who was a supporter of Monothelitism. He had both the pope and St. Maximus arrested in 653. The pope died in custody, but St. Maximus was brought to Constantinople for trial. He had his tongue cut out and right hand chopped off before being sent into exile, where he died soon after. Though a Greek, St. Maximus was unwavering in his support of the Church of Rome in the dispute with the Monothelitists and Emperor Constans. In explaining his position to his fellow bishops at Constantinople (many of whom chided him for siding with the pope against the emperor), St. Maximus wrote:

> For the very ends of the earth and those in every part of the world who purely and rightly confess the Lord, look directly to the most holy Church of the Romans and its confession and faith as though it were a sun of unfailing light, expecting from it the illuminating splendor of the Fathers and sacred dogmas. . . . For ever since the

Incarnate Word of God came down to us, all the churches
of Christians everywhere have held that greatest Church
there to be their sole base and foundation, since on the
one hand, it is in no way overcome by the gates of Hades,
according to the very promise of the Savior, but holds
the keys of the orthodox confession and faith in him
and opens the only true and real religion to those who
approach with godliness, and on the other hand, it shuts
up and locks every heretical mouth that speaks unrigh-
teousness against the most High.[8]

Photius

Schism would again rend the churches in the so-called Photian Schism of
863 to 867. This time, the issue was the question of whether the Byzantine
emperor had the right to depose and elevate patriarchs of Constantinople
without the approval of the pope. In 857, Emperor Michael III deposed
the patriarch Ignatius for political reasons and in his place elevated a layman named Photius.

Pope Nicholas condemned the appointment of Photius. The crisis was
exacerbated by conditions on the ground in Bulgaria, where the pagan
Bulgars were being evangelized simultaneously by Eastern and Western
missionaries—each with their own customs—and Constantinople and
Rome each claimed jurisdiction over the Bulgars. Photius attacked the
Latin missionaries over the use of *Filioque* in the creed—this is the phrase
"and the Son," referring to the procession of the Holy Spirit. This phrase
had been common in the West since the late patristic times but had never
been used in the East.

The patriarch took the unprecedented step of summoning a synod
in 867 and declaring the pope deposed and excommunicated, as well as

all in communion with him. Nicholas died before word of these actions reached him, and Photius was deposed soon after following a political coup. A council was summoned in Constantinople, declaring that Photius never was a bishop and invalidating all of his acts, including his defamatory writings against the pope. The great irony of the story is that Photius would later regain the episcopate of Constantinople a second time a decade later, this time in communion with Rome. The new pope, John VIII, agreed to recognize Photius as bishop in exchange for the Byzantine emperor's acknowledgment that the pope was the head of the universal Church.

Sibling Rivalry

As we can see, the relationship between the East and the West had been fraught with tension almost from the beginning. Of course, these tensions would boil over in what has become known as the Great Schism of 1054. That, however, does not fall within the parameters of this book. It is worth mentioning, however, that is has become common in contemporary Catholic literature to portray the differences between East and West as merely cultural, essentially based on ancient ethnic hostilities and mutual misunderstanding. While this may be true to some degree, we should not overlook the real differences between East and West—especially those that developed in the centuries after the Schism of 1054. Reunion with the East is not merely about getting over old hard feelings but about working out concrete theological solutions to disputes on subjects such as the authority of the pope, the nature of the episcopacy, and other matters that are purely theological.

YOU BE THE JUDGE:

Did the Eastern churches ever affirm the primacy of Rome?

To this day, Eastern Orthodox maintains that the Eastern churches had never affirmed the Roman primacy during the first millennium. However, as Pope Gregory the Great said, "Both the most pious lord the emperor and our brother the bishop . . . continually acknowledge" the supremacy of Rome.[9] An example of one of these acknowledgments is the *Formula of Hormisdas*, a statement sworn by Patriarch John II of Constantinople as a condition for ending the Acacian Schism in 519. The formula sworn by the patriarch states:

> Following . . . the Apostolic See in all things and proclaiming all its decisions, we endorse and approve all the letters which Pope St. Leo wrote concerning the Christian religion. And so I hope I may deserve to be associated with you in the one communion which the Apostolic See proclaims, in which the whole, true, and perfect security of the Christian religion resides. I promise that from now on those who are separated from the communion of the Catholic Church, that is, who are not in agreement with the Apostolic See, will not have their names read during the sacred mysteries.[10]

The Formula of Hormisdas is an excellent example of the historical Byzantine acknowledgment of Rome's preeminence.

Chapter 7

The Carolingian Renaissance

The Italian peninsula in the eighth century was a chaotic place. The popes had carved out what amounted to an independent dominion for themselves near Rome. Their lands, however, were constantly threatened by the Lombards, a Germanic tribe that had settled in northern Italy in the sixth century and initially converted from paganism to Arianism. They were always encroaching on papal lands and were generally hostile to the papacy. Though the early medieval popes had gradually assumed characteristics of secular monarchs, they seldom had much at their disposal in terms of military resources. If endangered, the popes had little recourse but to ask the emperors at Constantinople for aid. After all, the Byzantine emperors still claimed suzerainty over Italy, even if they could seldom enforce it.

But—as we have mentioned—by the eighth century, the popes had soured on the political and spiritual unreliability of Constantinople. They needed an ally much nearer, and one with whom they would have fewer arguments. The eighth-century popes found this ally in the Carolingian dynasty of the Franks. This alliance of the papacy with the Carolingian dynasty shaped the direction of Western Christianity for the remainder of the first millennium.

The Carolingians themselves owed their throne to the papacy. Recall that we have already discussed the Merovingians, the first Christian dynasty of France. By the eighth century, the successors of Clovis had been reduced to mere figureheads; real power in the kingdom was wielded by a small cadre of nobles known as the mayors of the palace. One of these mayors was Pepin the Short, the son of the famous Charles Martel of the

Carolingian house. In 751, Pepin wrote to Pope Zachary, to explain the state of things in France and the weakness of the Merovingian dynasty. He posed a very simple yet suggestive question to the pope: "With regard to the kings of the Franks who no longer possess the royal power: is this state of things proper?"[1] Pope Zachary responded that such a state was *not* proper. Whoever wielded power in fact, he stated, ought to be king in name as well. This response was all Pepin needed; he promptly deposed the last Merovingian, banished him to a monastery, and took the throne of France as King Pepin, the first Carolingian monarch.

A Gift to the Pope

Pepin was not long in repaying the debt he owed to the Church. In 754, King Pepin marched his armies into northern Italy to destroy the Lombard force there once and for all. After the Lombards were subdued, Pepin wrested their lands from them and bequeathed them to the new pope, Stephen II. These newly acquired lands ran in a diagonal strip across Italy from the Tyrrhenian Sea to the Adriatic. These lands would come to be known as the "Donation of Pepin" and were the foundation of the Papal States, the sovereign central Italian kingdom ruled by the popes for more than a thousand years. From 754 onward, the pope would be not only the spiritual head of Christendom but also the political ruler of an autonomous central Italian kingdom.

In summer of 754, Pope Stephen made the long trek to Paris to crown Pepin and his sons. It was the first recorded instance of the coronation of a king by a pope. This ushered in what would be known as the Carolingian era, a period that would last until 888 and is popularly viewed as a kind of "golden age" of Christianity's first millennium. Some scholars refer to this period as the "Carolingian Renaissance" to denote the marvelous development of literature, art, architecture, and education during the era.

Flourishing Together

The apex of the Carolingian era undoubtedly came during the reign of Pepin's son Charles, known popularly as Charles the Great or Charlemagne (r. 768–814). Charlemagne expanded Frankish power westward into Spain and as far east as Slovakia. In Germany he reduced the German Saxons—many of them still pagan—to vassalage. Like his father, he marched his army into Italy to protect the pope, for which he received a special gift from Pope Leo III on Christmas Day of the year 800. Charlemagne, while kneeling in prayer at St. Peter's Basilica, was approached by the pope who placed a crown on his head and proclaimed him "emperor of the Romans."

In doing this, Pope Leo was declaring Charlemagne the source of political unity for all Christians, the heir of the old Christian empire established by Constantine and his successors. The conferring of this title was also a snub to the Byzantines. They had held unbroken succession of the imperial title since the time of Constantine, but their authority in the West was practically nonexistent. This gesture became known as the *translatio imperii*, the "translation" of the imperial crown from the Byzantines to the Franks in the person of Charlemagne by the pope.

Our focus here is on the Church, so it is far beyond our scope to consider the theology of the *translatio imperii* theory, political history of the Carolingians, or even Charlemagne alone. The Church under the Carolingians flourished. Pepin, Charlemagne, and their successors considered themselves consecrated defenders of the Church with special ties to the papacy. They patronized education, endowed churches and abbeys, sponsored missionary ventures, and organized regional synods where the Church worked out doctrinal and disciplinary problems.

The relationship between the Church and the Carolingians was mutually beneficial: On the one hand, the Church received a stalwart defender, much more dependable than the Byzantines had been. On the other hand, the imperial title conferred by the pope gave the Carolingian monarchs a special sort of moral authority in the eyes of Western Christians. The throne and altar reinforced one another in the pursuit of their different (though parallel) aims. The Carolingian kingdom was seen to be a kind of holy reflection of the kingdom of heaven. God the Father, looking into the mirror, would see the reflection of the Carolingian emperor, his earthly parallel. An elaboration of this ideology is provided by the Irish scholar Hibernicus, who was one of Charlemagne's intellectual retinue: "There is only one who enthroned in the realm of the heavens. . . . It is proper that under him, one only be the ruler on earth, in merit an example to all men."[2]

Up Close and Personal:
THE FAITH OF CHARLEMAGNE

Though Charlemagne's later reputation as a saintly king and Christian sage was certainly exaggerated, it is true he was a very pious man who prayed regularly and labored to understand God's will. You can still see his throne in the chapel of Aachen where he was accustomed to hearing Mass daily. "He cherished with the greatest fervor and devotion the principles of the Christian religion,"[3] said Einhard, one of his biographers. The emperor was always willing to support the needy and engage in good works.

Like his imperial Byzantine counterparts, Charlemagne took an active hand in ecclesiastical affairs and summoned regional councils, such as the one at Frankfort in 794. He funded churches throughout his realm and donated lavishly to the papal court; again, Einhard says:

He . . . heaped its treasury with a vast wealth of gold, silver, and precious stones. He sent great and countless gifts to the popes, and throughout his whole reign the wish that he had nearest his heart was to re-establish the ancient authority of the city of Rome under his care and by his influence, and to defend and protect the Church of St. Peter, and to beautify and enrich it out of his own store above all other churches.[4]

Charlemagne frequently read the lives of the saints and was particularly fond of St. Augustine's *City of God*. Thus it was that in his works and his personal piety, Charlemagne set the standard for what a Christian king of the High Middle Ages should be.

Christian Education

One of the notable clerics of the early Carolingian era was the Anglo-Saxon monk Alcuin. Alcuin came to the court of Charlemagne at Aachen in 782 and assumed control over education in the Frankish palace. Alcuin's influence soon spread, and he was consulted by Charlemagne on all educational matters, becoming a sort of royal prime minister of education.

Acting on Alcuin's advice, Charlemagne inaugurated an educational reform throughout his empire. The centerpiece of this reform was the education of the clergy. Recognizing that most education happened under ecclesiastical auspices, Charlemagne enlisted bishops and monasteries as the agents of his reform. In his famous educational capitulary of 787, Charlemagne decreed:

> [We have] judged it to be of utility that, in their bishoprics and monasteries committed by Christ's favor to his charge, care should be taken that there should not only be a regular manner

of life, but also the study of letters, each to teach and learn them according to his ability and the Divine assistance. . . . Let there, therefore, be chosen [for the work of teaching] men who are both willing and able to learn and let them apply themselves to this work with a zeal equal to the earnestness with which we recommend it to them.[5]

Another decree of 789 ordered, "Let every monastery and every abbey have its school, in which boys may be taught the Psalms, the system of musical notation, singing, arithmetic and grammar."[6]

These monastery schools provided education for not only aspiring clerics and wards of the nobility but also the country children from the local villages. Charlemagne envisioned a Christian education available to all children of his domain, regardless of social status. To secure this worthy goal, a capitulary of 796 commands that education be provided gratis:

[We command that] the priests establish schools in every town and village, and if any of the faithful wish to entrust their children to them to learn letters, that they refuse not to accept them but with all charity teach them . . . and let them exact no price from the children for their teaching nor receive anything from them save what parents may offer voluntarily and from affection.[7]

Monastic Reform

Monasticism also underwent a thorough reform in Charlemagne's empire. By the time Charlemagne became emperor, it had been more than 250 years since St. Benedict composed his *Rule*. Though Benedictine monasticism remained dominant in the West, its observance varied greatly from place to place. St. Benedict's Rule had originally left a great deal to the discretion of abbots. Over the years, many monasteries had become accustomed to exercising that discretion in favor of easing disciplines, such that the Rule was often not observed as St. Benedict envisioned.

This situation would be rectified by another holy Benedict, St. Benedict of Aniane. Born Witiza (747–821), he was the son of a Frankish count close to the Carolingian family. As a nobleman, Witiza was destined for the life of a warrior in the ranks of Charlemagne. In 773, however, he had a brush with death in combat that caused him to rethink his priorities. He decided to abandon the martial life and devote himself to God as a Benedictine.

Witiza took the name Benedict, after the founder of the order who had inspired him in his renunciation of the world. It did not take long before St. Benedict realized that many Benedictine monks were no longer keeping the Rule of St. Benedict with the same rigor as the original Benedictines. To remedy this, he founded a monastery at a place called Aniane dedicated to the strict observance of the Rule.

This monastery became an inspiration to reform-minded Benedictines across France and soon became a model for monastic discipline. Other monasteries began imitating the practices of Aniane. The son of Charlemagne, Louis the Pious (r. 813–840), was an enthusiastic supporter of St. Benedict of Aniane's vision. He summoned two royal synods that commanded the monasteries within Carolingian lands to adopt the disciplines there; St. Benedict himself was empowered by imperial decree to ensure the monasteries complied with the reforms. By the time St. Benedict of Aniane died in 821, he had overseen the greatest reform of Western monasticism since St. Benedict of Nursia and set Western monasticism on a trajectory it would follow for the next century.

The Roman Rite

It is also to the Carolingians that we owe the spread of the Roman Rite to become the dominant liturgy of the West. The story of the growth of the

Roman liturgy during the Carolingian era is fascinating and complex; regrettably we will not be able to give it the full treatment it deserves. We can, however, sketch a basic outline of its development.

When the Franks overran Gaul in the fifth century, the existing Roman liturgy was mixed with various Gallic elements, creating a kind of hybrid Romano-Frankish liturgy. By the eighth century this hybrid liturgy had developed several problems. Adaptations from local custom had crept in to such a degree that there really was no one "rite" but a diversity of regional rites. The proliferation of variations meant a corresponding proliferation of liturgical texts that were often mistranslated or corrupted.

In 754, King Pepin ordered that his realm adopt the Roman liturgy as celebrated in Rome—that is, a "pure" Roman liturgy divested of the regional variations. This had the benefit of not only solidifying ties with Rome but also promoting cultural and political unity. The decree met with limited success, however. Though it was not difficult to mandate the use of Roman liturgical books, the Roman liturgy was particularly suited to the culture of Rome and could not be easily transplanted to Frankish lands with their own unique customs.

Charlemagne continued his father's work by requesting Pope Hadrian send him a "pure" sacramentary to be used as a model for all Frankish liturgies. This text, known as the *Hadrianum*, was ill suited for parish use, being more of a ritual for papal Masses that were far too elaborate for Charlemagne's needs. Charlemagne entrusted the revision of this text to none other than St. Benedict of Aniane, who amended the *Hadrianum* extensively. Benedict added texts for Sunday Masses that had been omitted, as well as texts for important vigils, weekday Masses, consecrations of clerics and women religious, ordinations for minor orders, and much more. Most of these revisions were taken from older sacramentaries already in possession of the Frankish church.

The resulting liturgy was still something of a hybrid compared to the liturgies used at Rome. Still, it was much closer to the unified and universal rite that Pepin and Charlemagne desired. This rite gradually prevailed across Europe wherever Carolingian power extended.

Charlemagne also wanted Roman church music. To that end, he sent his best cantors to the papal court to learn the Roman chants. These chants were standardized across the Carolingian Empire, facilitating the spread of Gregorian chant across Europe.

The reforms of Pepin and Charlemagne forever wedded western Europe to the Roman rite, a unity that would be maintained for over a thousand years. Though certain regions maintained their own local liturgies—the Ambrosian rite in the area around Milan, the Mozarabic rite of Visigothic Spain, and the various usages of medieval England—by and large the Carolingian reforms brought liturgical uniformity to the West.

Waning Power and New Settlers

Like any other dynasty, eventually the power of the Carolingians began to wane. After the death of Charlemagne's son Louis the Pious in 840, the three grandsons of Charlemagne jostled for control of the empire. The strife proved inconclusive, however, and in 843 the three brothers agreed to the Treaty of Verdun, a plan to split the empire into three: France in the west, Germany in the east, and a middle kingdom called "Lotharingia," which would subsequently be gobbled up by its neighbors on either side.

The Carolingian monarchs of France became less impressive with each successive generation. We can see this in the progressive devolution of their nicknames: Louis the Pious, Charles the Bald, Charles the Fat, Louis the Stammerer, and finally Charles the Simple. In the middle ninth century, the pagan Vikings began attacking northern France. Perceiving the Franks to be weak, they stepped up their assaults, even laying siege to Paris twice in 845 and in 885.

A Danish warlord named Rollo spent the last quarter of the ninth century pillaging northern France. Both Charles the Bald and Charles the Simple were unable to push him out. In 911, Rollo attacked Chartres. He was beaten back by Robert, the count of Paris, but the French were so weary of fighting that Charles the Simple offered Rollo and his Vikings extensive lands in northern France to settle if Rollo would convert to Christianity and promise to fight for Charles. Rollo was accordingly baptized, along with his men, and settled in northern France. Rollo was made a duke in Charles's kingdom; his people became known as Normans (for "Northmen," signifying their origin in Scandinavia). The duchy of Rollo became known as Normandy, and its capital was established at Rouen.

The conversion of Rollo and the Normans would prove to have profound consequences for Europe and the Church. The Normans embraced Catholicism with exceptional zeal. In the following century, it would be the Normans who spearheaded the movement known as the Crusades. The architectural and artistic reform known as the "Gothic style" also came out of Normandy, with cities like Rouen, Caen, and Le Havre becoming the earliest homes of the ecclesiastical architecture that would come to identify the Catholic Church in the Middle Ages.

It is hard to overemphasize the importance of the Carolingian era in the history of the Church. Whether we consider liturgy, music, evangelization, monasticism, or literature, the Carolingian epoch stands out as the apex of the first millennium. Though the Carolingian dynasty ended in France in 987, later generations of Christians would always look back to the reign of Charlemagne as a golden age of faith and culture. Charlemagne in particular was venerated as the ideal Christian monarch. Literature of latter ages presented him as a holy sage, full of wisdom and mighty in the Holy Spirit. In the medieval epic *Song of Roland*, Charlemagne is presented as two hundred years old with a flowing white beard and a quasi-sacramental power, a veritable priest-king of old. While we may chuckle at these historical embellishments, they point to the fundamental truth

that later generations of medieval people recognized how very important the Carolingian period was for the development of the Church and
Christian society.

YOU BE THE JUDGE:

Wasn't the Church consumed with worry over the spread of Islam?

One of the greatest sociopolitical forces of the first Christian
millennium was emergence of Islam in the seventh century. In
the one hundred years following the death of Mohammed in
632, Islamic armies devoured half of Christendom—Byzantine
Syria, the Holy Land, Byzantine territories in North Africa, and
Visigothic Spain all fell before the crescent banner. The Islamic
armies even crossed the Pyrenees into France, halted only by
the fortitude of the Frankish leader Charles Martel, who crushed
them at Tours in 732 and stopped a century of Islamic expansion.

Faced with the loss of so many lands, wasn't the Church
consumed with worry over Islamic growth? Why didn't Church
leaders call for organized, multinational resistance to Islamic
aggression as they would later do at the time of the First
Crusade?

There are various answers. For one thing, it took Christians
some time to understand exactly what Islam was. The earliest
Christian work addressing Islam was *The Fountain of Knowledge*
by St. John of Damascus (d. 749). St. John called Islam "the heresy of the Ishmaelites"[8] and seems to have considered it a Christian heresy, just another in a long line of heresies that had always
plagued the Church. It took Christians some time to understand
the unique existential threat posed by Islam.

Another issue was that the papacy of the seventh and eighth centuries did not wield anything close to the sort of influence it did at the time of the Crusades. By the time Pope Urban II called the First Crusade in 1095, the popes had spent centuries centralizing their control over the Church, successfully faced down the Holy Roman emperors, and were universally acknowledged as the ultimate moral authority of the West. But such was not the case in the seventh century. Papal authority was much more localized. Bishops and dioceses were much more independent. The Papal States did not even exist yet. Even had some energetic pope tried to summon something like a crusade, he would have lacked the influence necessary to organize it.

We must also remember that in the seventh century there was not a firmly established ideal of "Christian Europe" enshrined in popular consciousness. Consider that in the very year Martel was fighting to keep the Muslims out of France (732), the majority of Germany was still pagan. Swaths of England and Scotland were still pagan. Scandinavia was entirely pagan. The Balkans would be pagan for another two hundred years. Christians did not rise up and fight for Christian Europe because Christian Europe itself didn't exist yet. Rather, there was a smattering of Christian and pagan kingdoms existing side by side; sometimes Christian and pagan populations intermingled within a single kingdom. The prospect of Europe being hemmed in by heathens did not alarm the Church because it had always been hemmed in by heathens.

We may of course presume that bishops and popes lamented the loss of Christian lands. But in the seventh to eighth centuries, it was primarily laymen with political-military goals who made the most determined stands against Islam—men like Charles Martel, Odo of Aquitaine, or Pelayo of Asturias. The age of popes uniting the kingdoms of Christendom under the banner of the cross to do battle against the infidel was still some time off.

Chapter 8

Imperium and Sacerdotium

As the Church grew throughout the early Middle Ages, it became more influential in society. This influence was expressed in many ways. The Church's pastors were moral leaders in their communities. A holy monk, nun, or eloquent bishop could sway public opinion on an issue if they thought the good of the Church required it.

The Church was also influential due to the amount of land it owned. By the time Charlemagne was crowned emperor, vast tracts of land across Europe were administered by the Church: monastic establishments, cathedral grounds, parish properties, or agricultural lands under ecclesiastical governance, such as large swaths of Sicily and the Papal States.

Another avenue of influence was the tie that bound the Church to the royal court in the kingdoms of Christendom. Kings often took bishops or monks as advisors—such as Alcuin to Charlemagne or St. Isidore to King Reccared. Because of their learning and reputation, such men often served in a diplomatic capacity and could be instrumental in shaping royal policy.

With so much influence coalescing within the Church, it is not surprising that lay authorities tried to bring it under their control. After the fall of Rome, the Church was the most organized institution in western Europe and its ranks were composed of the most educated men of the age. A king who could successfully bend the Church to his will within his kingdom held a valuable resource. Conversely, a king at odds with the Church was inviting discord into his realm.

Manipulating the Church

An enterprising ruler had many ways he could manipulate the Church. The most obvious method was by land grants. As populations converted to Christianity, land was required for churches and monasteries. This land was a lord's to grant, and it came with the understanding that the Church would support the king or lord in his policies, insofar as they did not contravene the Church's traditions. This exchange could best be described as a kind of patronage—land in exchange for support. In the High Middle Ages, this support would be further formalized into the concept of fealty, whereby the bishop or abbot literally swore obedience to the lord as part of obtaining title to ecclesiastical lands.

Another common practice was the spread of the commendatory system. The history of the commendatory system is too long to delve into here, its roots going back to the patristic era. We can, however, note that by the early Carolingian era it was common for monastic establishments to be held *in commendam*, which meant that the temporal management of the property was "commended" to a layman appointed by the ruler. The layman generally took no care for the spiritual well-being of the monks. He often managed the abbey's revenues solely for his own benefit, fleecing the monks and dividing the spoils between himself and the king. Many monasteries were driven into ruin by this mismanagement, but even those that weren't were compelled to acquiesce passively to this arrangement if they hoped to gain even partial access to their revenues.

Choosing Bishops

By far the easiest and most effective way lay authorities manipulated the Church was through control of episcopal appointments. Of course, lay rulers never claimed for themselves the right to create a bishop directly. The ordination of a bishop is an exercise of the Sacrament of Holy Orders and as such can only be conferred by other bishops. But the king might claim the right to choose the man upon whom this ordination was conferred, and this was often the case.

This practice took many forms. Sometimes a slate of candidates might be put forward for the king to choose from, a kind of compromise whereby the Church had ultimate say over the slate, but the king got to select his favorite. On other occasions the Church actively sought out the king to render a decision ("Whom does the king wish to fill this episcopal vacancy?"); sometimes the king himself took initiative and made his will known unilaterally ("This is the man I want in that diocese"). In some instances the Church was free to ordain whomever it wished, but the king might retain a veto power in the case of objectionable candidates. A very common arrangement was for the king to confer with a council of notable ecclesiastics in his realm and choose a bishop by a kind of consensus between himself and the clergy. Missionary bishops establishing new churches in pagan lands usually came at the behest of both the lay and the religious authorities. When St. Boniface came into Germany in 723 to begin his missionary work, he bore letters of authorization from both the Frankish ruler Charles Martel and Pope Gregory II.

Given the important role of the Church and the political ambitions of secular rules, it is not surprising that such a system emerged. What is surprising is how well it generally worked during the Dark Ages. While there were always occasional bad apples, in general the episcopacy of the Dark Ages fared much better in the court of public opinion than the bishops of the High Middle Ages and later. The literary trope of the wicked, worldly bishop comes from a much later age. However they were chosen, most bishops of the Dark Ages seemed to have been simple men of modest learning and great piety genuinely concerned with the salvation of souls and the good of the Church. Having such men filling the episcopal sees of Europe benefitted everybody, whether lay or clergy.

Of course, the system could be abused. The Fifth Council of Orleans in 549 stipulated that bishops in Merovingian France were to be appointed *cum voluntate regis*, that is, "with the will of the king." This led to immediate abuses with the episcopal office becoming increasingly politicized. The Third Council of Paris in 557 tried to crush the abuse, but the practice of royal approval went on unopposed. Charles Martel, grandfather of Charlemagne, was one of the worst abusers of the privilege; Charlemagne continued it, albeit in a manner more acceptable to the Church. In general, the system became more prone to abuse as the fledgling kingdoms of Europe grew in power and organization. An excellent example of this is furnished by the Church's experience with the Holy Roman Empire.

Otto and the Holy Roman Empire

By the late ninth century, the Carolingian Empire that Charlemagne had forged was in desperate straits. His successors followed the politically suicidal Frankish custom of dividing their lands up among their heirs; the Treaty of Verdun in 843 delineated what realms would be ruled by whom. The so-called Middle Kingdom of Lothair was picked apart by its larger rivals to the east and west. Soon there appeared an "East Frankish" and a "West Frankish" realm, which would go on to become France and Germany. The last Carolingians to hold these offices died in 987 and 911, respectively.

In the east, in the Frankish holdings of Saxony and the German dukedoms, authority fell to the local nobles. After much civil discord, Otto I of Saxony was crowned king in 936 and emperor by the pope John XII in 962. The imperial coronation of Otto and his German successors is considered the beginning of the so-called Holy Roman Empire.

At the time of Otto's coronation, the prevailing understanding of German kingship was that the king was only the highest lord in a network of lords and vassals. Beyond that, he held little power that was not honorary or ceremonial. Real power was vested in the body of dukes who had exercised authority ever since late Roman times. The ducal office was hereditary and thus ensured that any king would always have powerful opponents who presented a check to his power.

Otto, however, was not content with a merely honorary kingship. He took Charlemagne as his model and exploited to the fullest the prevailing attitudes toward sacred kingship in order to strengthen his position. First, Otto was crowned king at Aachen instead of his native Saxony, thus evoking all the connections with Charlemagne. But the most decisive action he took against the power of the dukes was his use of ecclesiastical persons to fill vacant secular positions, supplanting the entrenched nobility with bishops and abbots. This was a decision that would have profound ramifications for the Church as well as his empire.

Otto's program had three advantages: First, since the clergy was celibate, they had no offspring to pass on their titles to, and thus the offices could not take on a hereditary nature. Second, because they took office by appointment and not inheritance, they owed their position to Otto personally and were thus likely to be more loyal. Third, clerics were highly educated, or at least literate, which is more than can be said of most of the German dukes of the tenth century. This ensured a faithful, educated administration that could be switched around or altered if the king so chose, and so it provided him with a bulwark against the recalcitrant dukes.

Secular Meddling

Otto did not "appoint" bishops in the direct sense but manipulated their elections by requiring his assent to their appointment. As we have seen, he was doing nothing novel; since Roman times such arrangement with the secular authority had been common. By Otto's time, royal intervention in episcopal elections was a well-established royal prerogative grounded in the monarch's role as guardian of the Church in his realm. For at least two centuries there had never been a time when the Western kings and emperors did not exercise an arbitrary control over the candidates for the episcopacy.

It is fair to ask why the Church tolerated this secular interference. The answer is surprising. The clergy of Carolingian and Ottonian times did not fight the royal prerogative because they were quite happy with it. It provided an excellent opportunity for the exercise of ecclesiastical influence at court. A bishop who received an appointment from Otto could wield a considerable amount of clout with the king on behalf of his diocese. And the kings were happy to throw their weight behind the Church as well, as both a political tool and an act of personal piety. So long as able and faithful bishops were appointed there was little cause for complaint. The clergy did not contest the infringement upon their canonical rights because it was more desirable that their bishop wield influence at court. Under Otto, the Church felt itself to be regaining its dignity and authority.

Otto's innovation was not in that he meddled in episcopal appointments. Rather, it was the systematic, calculating method by which he did so. Never before had so extensive a program of politically motivated episcopal appointments been undertaken, and never so methodically. But Otto had in mind nothing other than the complete subordination of the German princes to himself, and the widespread use of the royal prerogative in episcopal elections was the surest way to accomplish this.

Role Reversal

Once Otto was crowned Holy Roman emperor in 962, he further extended his power by claiming—on his authority as emperor and temporal lord of the Christian realm—the right to approve papal elections as well. The papacy was understandably unhappy with this situation, but it had little choice. Like Pepin and Charlemagne before him, Otto had marched into Italy at the behest of Pope John XII with the purpose of freeing Rome from the control of a usurper. Before Otto agreed to this, however, he extracted the "Ottonian privilege" from the papacy, an oath stating that a new pope could never be elected without the permission of himself or his son. John XII reluctantly assented in order to win Otto's military aid.

This was a natural consequence of Otto's interference in German epis-copal elections. If the Church was to serve the crown, which was Otto's desire, then the Church must be under royal authority, which meant that the papacy had to be bent to serve the will of the Holy Roman emperor. Remember that the prevailing ideology since the Carolingian times had been that the emperor was the earthly parallel to God, the emperor of heaven. Essentially, the original arrangement Leo III made with Charle-magne had backfired. Leo III crowned Charlemagne to demonstrate that the imperial dignity of the Carolingians came not from themselves but from the papacy, who had the authority to "translate" it from the Greeks to the Franks. Otto, however, used this same claim to assert that the Holy Roman emperor, by his divine appointment, had a special guardianship over the Church that no other prince did. He accomplished this by virtue of the very same privilege Leo III had thought would keep the emperors beholden to will of the papacy!

We are not interested here in Otto's long and tumultuous political career. Our focus is on how Otto altered the balance between the *impe-rium* and the *sacerdotium*, that is, between the powers of the state and the clergy. Otto's belief that the imperial title gave him a protectorship over the Church of Rome was extremely consequential. Previous kings had applied this ideology to their own local churches, but Otto was the first to apply it to the Church of Rome itself, at least explicitly. This would prove calamitous for the papacy. Furthermore, though his control of episcopal appointments benefited his imperial administration, such an arrangement could not be good for the Church's spiritual mission in the long term. Even though Otto was solicitous to choose capable bishops for his government, the demands of government necessarily detracted from time spent attending to spiritual matters, which were farmed out to lower and less competent clerics. Otto enmeshed temporal and spiritual lordship so tightly that it would take another three hundred years of vigorous debate to trace out the boundaries of each. The Investiture Controversy of the eleventh century would largely erupt as an attempt to undo Otto's creation. It could be said that the Protestant Reformation was another.

A Christian King in England

Across the English Channel, between the time of the Carolingians and the Ottonians, another house of Germanic origin, the Anglo-Saxon house of Wessex, was uniting the petty kingdoms of England under its authority. This would not be so extraordinary in itself, but the personage of its greatest king, Alfred (r. 871–899), stands out as an exemplary example of what we might call Christian theocratic kingship, for we see in King Alfred a fusion of religious and political leadership.

Most of what is known about Alfred personally comes from his biographer, the Welsh monk Asser. From him we know that Alfred consciously modeled his understanding of his kingship on that of Charlemagne and his court. Alfred perhaps goes even further than Charlemagne, for, as we shall see, he claimed a status that is almost sacramental. Though Asser should be taken with a grain of salt as royal propagandist of sorts, nevertheless the picture of Alfred that emerges from his pages is one of an authentically good and pious ruler who desired the sincere well-being of his people and the Church. While Otto's dealings with the Church were deliberately manipulative, Alfred's motives seem to have been more pious. In Alfred we see lay influence over the Church at its best. It is hard not to feel some kind of personal admiration for this sincere yet powerful Dark Age king.

The Anglo-Saxons (like the continental Saxons from whom Otto sprung) did not see a strict separation between temporal and spiritual law. The king was the overseer of both. Hence, we see Alfred calling assemblies of nobles to debate matters of importance, but he just as frequently called synods of bishops to formulate ecclesiastical policy—quite often the attendees were the same at each. Whatever the clergy thought of this, Alfred saw little distinction between the two types of gatherings. When the king sought the opinions of his vassals on secular issues, they were called an assembly; if on holy matters, then they were a synod. This assembly, whether it was discharging religious or secular affairs, was commonly referred to as the king's *witan*. Church and state affairs were quite intentionally mingled.

Although he did not know how to read or write until later in life, Alfred was one of the most educated kings of the Saxon era. He valued education highly and was exceptionally pious. It was his practice to hear Mass daily, recite the divine office, pray at night, give alms, and hear the scriptures read to him. Asser, following a common convention in describing medieval kings, said that King Alfred "resembled the pious and most wise and rich Solomon, king of the Hebrews."[1] The king carried about on his person a small book filled with his favorite prayers that he had heard from the daily readings, which he had Asser or some other attendant read to him at times.

It is no surprise that Alfred insisted on the education of his clergy and his lords. Charlemagne, too, had promoted literacy, but Alfred took it a step further. Asser gives us the humorous picture of Alfred educating the children of his vassals in a makeshift schoolhouse set up in his palace while he forced the uncouth Saxon lords to try their hand at reading and writing. He also fostered education among the clergy, which probably simply meant making sure they could read and write in both Latin and Anglo-Saxon. He believed this mandate to educate stemmed from his place as the God-ordained king, and the whole enterprise took on a religious nature. As Asser puts it, God "stirred up the mind of the king by inward working."[2] Education was God's business.

Like most medieval Christians, Alfred fervently believed that the devotion and righteousness of the king had a profound impact on the welfare of the kingdom. Alfred had a personal experience of this principle from the reign of his older brother, King Ethelred, at the Battle of Ashdown in 871. Alfred was a young commander at this battle and regarded the Christian victory against the pagan Danes as nothing short of miraculous. The English armies were being beaten back, and the presence of King Ethelred was urgently requested on the battlefield. Asser records what happened:

> For his brother, King Ethelred, was still in his tent, praying
> fervently and hearing Mass, and he stoutly declared that he
> would not depart thence alive until the priest had made an end
> of saying Mass, for he would not abandon the service of God
> for that of man. So did he, and the faith of this Christian king
> availed much with the Lord.[3]

Alfred, out in the thick of the battle, was suddenly strengthened and reformed his men's position. Alfred drew his shield wall together in order and attacked. The English pushed the Danes back and scored a major victory, which Asser, Alfred, and the entire English people attributed to the piety of King Ethelred.

When Alfred later became king, he did not shirk functions that most Catholics today would describe as sacramental. In an extreme exercise of this quasi-sacramental character, Asser reports how the Danish king Guthrum, upon defeat, agreed to accept Christianity and was baptized personally by King Alfred. This is the most extreme case of a king exercising sacramental authority—perhaps second only to the passage in the *Song of Roland* that depicts Charlemagne pronouncing a formula of absolution.

Alfred, overall, enjoyed a long and prosperous reign and always held fast to the idea that his kingly lordship was given by the power of God; an English subject could best be a good Christian by being a good vassal. Lordship, for Alfred, was the power that bound together the political world and, through a hierarchy of authority, connected the temporal world with the spiritual. God was at the apex of this chain of lordship, but immediately below God, without any intermediary, was the king.

Up Close and Personal:
KING ALFRED THE GREAT

Did you know that King Alfred personally undertook the translation of several Latin works into Anglo-Saxon? Though these translations were probably overseen by an assembly of learned monks, Asser attributes the translating the Alfred himself. It was well known that Alfred was barely literate, but Asser gets around this problem by saying that he translated "by the inspiration of God, [beginning] first to read and interpret at the same time on one and the same day."[4] Among Alfred's translations was the *Pastoral Care* of Pope St. Gregory the Great and a little-known work by St. Augustine called the *Soliloquies*, which consists of a dialogue of a man with his own soul. The amusing thing about his translations is the manner in which he rephrases classical or biblical ideas into the context of Anglo-Saxon culture. For example, Christ's commandment to "Love your neighbor as yourself" is translated as "Love your lord as you would love Christ himself."

Patron of the Church

Earlier, we mentioned grants of land and endowments of monasteries as two ways kings exercised influence over the Church. Alfred was no exception. He followed the typical Carolingian pattern of funding monasteries (he built a very famous one at Athelney), patronizing churches, disposing of church lands as he saw fit, and spending on lavish ecclesiastical building projects.

In every way Alfred was absolute lord of both the temporal and the spiritual realms, though he took this responsibility very seriously and never forgot that the king himself was accountable to a higher Lord. He took it upon himself to make sure that his vassals and clergy were up to the highest standards possible (or at least the highest possible for ninth-century Anglo-Saxon England). Furthermore, the English people, clergy and laity alike, loved Alfred for his efforts and gladly ceded to him the authority that he claimed for himself. No Anglo-Saxon bishop called Alfred to account over his disposal of Church lands. Nobody had to remind him of his obligations to God. Rather, it was King Alfred who exhorted the clergy of his realm to be better pastors.

Alfred represented the pinnacle of the English Anglo-Saxon period. Anglo-Saxon England would eventually fall to internal and external pressures, and fall to the Normans in 1066. The new Norman rulers would appropriate the old ideals of theocratic monarchy, but by that time things had changed.

The Papacy in Decline

We cannot pass on from this subject without mentioning the especially deleterious consequences lay domination of the Church had on the papacy in particular. The age of increased lay control of the Church corresponds with a period in papal history that historians often refer to as the *Saeculum obscurum*, literally the "Dark Age." Scholars debate how long the period lasted; some place it from 904 to 964, while others extend it from 867 to 1049. The specifics need not concern us. It is sufficient to know that the last few centuries of the first millennium were very bad years for the Church of Rome and are generally known as the nadir of the papacy.

We do not have the space to trace out the entire sordid history of the papacy during this period. We shall have to content ourselves with a general sketch of the epoch spiced up with a few examples.

The political wrangling of the Carolingians and Ottonians often spilled over into the papal court. An emperor might insist on a particular candidate against the express wishes of the Roman clergy. For example, in the papal conclave of 855 the Roman clergy elected Benedict III to the papacy. The Carolingian emperor, Louis II, opposed the election of Benedict and instead put forward his own candidate, Anastasius, the son of one of his supporters. Anastasius was installed by force, and Benedict was imprisoned. Popular sentiment was with Benedict, however, and Anastasius was regarded as an antipope. Eventually Benedict was released from prison and acknowledged as the rightful pope.

Popes often chose to support whatever imperial candidate seemed least likely to give them trouble, which could ironically lead to even more trouble. In 892, the reigning emperor Guy of Spoleto compelled Pope Formosus to crown his son and heir Lambert as co-emperor. Formosus, however, felt threatened by the aggression of Guy and invited a rival, Arnulf of Carinthia, to march into Italy and receive the imperial crown. Arnulf, Formosus, and Guy all soon died, leaving Lambert the undisputed imperial claimant. Lambert, understandably furious at the late pontiff's snubbing of his father, supported the election of Stephen VI, an opponent of Formosus, to the papacy. Stephen condemned the late pope posthumously by digging up his corpse and putting it on trial. Formosus was found guilty of various charges, his blessing finger was cut off, and the corpse was thrown into the Tiber River. This was the infamous Cadaver Synod of 897.

Lay domination of the papacy did not always come from distant kings and emperors. In the tenth century, the papacy found itself enmeshed with the affairs of a local family, the Theophylacti, those of the house of Theophylactus, count of Tusculum. Theophylactus was a powerful lord who ruled as virtual ruler of Rome from 905 to 924. His family held most of the important political offices in Rome, and the women of the family were deeply involved in the papal court through a web of conspiracies and affairs. For example, Theophylactus's daughter Marzonia became the concubine of Pope Sergius III at age fifteen and later became the mistress of John X. When Pope John and Marzonia had a falling out, she orchestrated his deposition and later had him murdered in prison. Through her influence, she was able to ensure that her bastard son by Pope Sergius was himself elected Pope John XI in 931. Now we see why this period is considered a Dark Age of the papacy!

Regents of God

The period of the Carolingians and Ottonians and the reign of the Wessex kings, from roughly about 768 to 1066, was the high point of sacerdotal kingship in the Middle Ages. During this time, kings and emperors freely manipulated clergy positions and vacancies in Church and secular lands to fit their agenda. They were openly acknowledged as the chief regents of God on earth, and the clergy generally accepted their meddling, reluctantly or enthusiastically depending on the ruler's relationship with the Church. Kings built churches and endowed abbeys, and in return expected the humble obedience of the clergy, who were simply regarded as vassals, albeit with a special clerical status. The relationship between the *imperium* and the *sacerdotium* had grown unbalanced in favor of the *imperium*.

By the eleventh century, however, things were beginning to change. A great educational and moral revival was taking place in the Church, flowing from the monastery of Cluny in France. New ideas would be developed about the relationship between Church and state, king and bishop. The Church would take the first steps out from under the shadow of royal control; the result was a bitter struggle between those who supported the traditional system and those who advocated Church autonomy. This struggle would rock the entire continent, but Germany and England in particular. History remembers it as the Investiture Controversy. We will touch on this later, but first we must pause and take a pleasant detour to survey the development of sacramental theology throughout the Dark Ages.

YOU BE THE JUDGE:

Do bad popes disprove papal infallibility?

The popes of the latter Dark Ages are widely considered to be some of the worst men to ever govern the Catholic Church. Men like Stephen VI (who presided over the Cadaver Synod of Pope Formosus), John XII (who gave church lands to his mistress, murdered several people, and was killed by a man who caught him in bed with his wife), and Benedict IX (who won the papacy by bribery and then resigned it to marry his mistress) tainted the papacy with scandal and infamy.

Such stories might seem at odds with the Catholic Church's teaching that the pope is infallible when he teaches definitively on matters of faith and morals that must be believed by the whole Church. How can we have confidence that a pope will teach the faith without fail when we have seen popes from history demonstrate such obvious and egregious moral failings?

We must remember that though the Holy Spirit guarantees to protect the pope from teaching error, it is a very limited power that applies only in very specific circumstances—that is, when the pope, in his capacity as pope, intends to define a matter of faith and morals that must be definitively held by the entire Church. Papal infallibility is nothing like a guarantee that the pope will never sin, or make a bad judgment, or even be a depraved criminal. The Church is divinely constituted and enjoys certain divine protections, but ultimately it is composed of fallible humans who are capable of making very human mistakes and committing very human sins.

The conditions upon which a pope is guaranteed to speak infallibly are narrow, while the number of ways he can go astray are many. This is why the Church always enjoins the faithful to pray for the pope—that he may be filled with prudence, zeal, and holiness. While the stories of the popes of the latter Dark Ages may be scandalous and regrettable, they do not disprove the Church's belief in the infallible teaching authority of the successor of Peter, as infallibility was never meant to be understood with reference to a pope's private moral life.

Chapter 9

Sacramental Controversies

We have seen the growth of the early medieval Church in terms of evangelization, that is, the geographical spread of Christianity into new lands. While this is undoubtedly an important part of the Church's story, it still remains only a part. We must also explore the Church's internal development. An excellent point of reference from which to consider this is the development of some of the Church's sacraments between the late patristic era and the High Middle Ages.

From apostolic times, some of the Church's sacramental rites had been passed down in very specific detail. These sacraments are called sacraments *in specie*. Examples include Baptism and Eucharist. From ancient times the elements of each sacrament were very clear: water (Baptism) and bread and wine (Eucharist). The prayers necessary to confect these sacraments, what would later be known as the sacramental "form," were also clearly established.

But other sacramental rites were not so fleshed out. These sacraments are called sacraments *in genera*. This means that, in general, the Church knew that the correct form and matter were present within the rite, but the Church could not identify exactly where. In some cases, theologians were not even in agreement on what the proper elements of a given sacrament were. The understanding and administration of these sacraments developed considerably over the centuries.

Sacramental Marriage

The best example of this is matrimony. The sacramental character of marriage had been understood since patristic times. St. Augustine wrote, "Among all people and all men the good that is secured by marriage consists in the offspring and in the chastity of married fidelity; but, in the case of God's people, it consists moreover in the holiness of the sacrament."[1] But there was a long list of lingering questions about what the sacrament consisted of exactly. At what moment was a couple actually married? Was it when they pronounced the vows? When they offered inner consent? When the marriage was consummated after the ceremony? And who conferred the sacrament? Was it an act of the man in "taking" the woman as wife? Was it bestowed by the Church in the person of the minister? Did the man and wife confer it on themselves? If the sacrament was brought about by the words of the vows, did it matter what specific words were spoken? Could cousins marry each other? If so, within what degrees was it permitted? Did the Church's minister need to physically witness the marriage, or was it sufficient that it merely take place in front of any witnesses and the Church be notified of it? And if the ceremony needed witnesses, how many witnesses sufficed?

Obviously these questions were complicated by the fact that marriage brought about a social reality, a new family. It was therefore imperative to understand exactly when a new family had been brought into existence. For example, suppose a man and woman wed but the man repudiated the woman before consummating the marriage on the wedding night. Had the couple been truly married if there was no consummation? Was their consent enough to bring about the sacrament, or was consummation necessary as well? These seemingly theoretical questions had very real applications.

Medieval theologians eventually settled on the idea that the form of the sacrament consisted in the consent offered by the two parties but witnessed by a minister of the Church. Later in the Middle Ages, the Fourth Lateran Council would further refine this by requiring other witnesses beside the minister.

We must note that the Church's teaching that marriage was brought about by the *mutual* consent of the parties was probably the single greatest advancement of women's status in the first millennium. Mutual consent meant that a woman's decision to marry was ultimately her own. She could no longer simply be "given" away by her father, as in pagan times. She must freely offer her consent or else no Christian marriage was possible. To be sure, familial pressure, financial concerns, and social convention were still tremendous considerations in whom a woman married. Nevertheless, the Church's insistence that a woman freely consent to marriage was an unequivocal affirmation of a woman's inherent personal dignity.

Sacramental Confession

The sacrament of confession also underwent an extraordinary development throughout the Dark Ages. To appreciate its evolution, we must first say a bit about how the sacrament of confession was administered at the close of the patristic era. Then we shall examine why and how the sacrament changed into something approximating more to what we recognize today.

In the late patristic era, as today, the sacrament of confession was meant to deal with grave sins committed after Baptism. This, however, is where the similarity ends, for though it had always been understood that confession was meant for the absolution of postbaptismal sins, exactly how and under what circumstances this sacrament was administered were more a matter of custom.

For example, confession in those days was reserved for sins of exceptional gravity. This would typically be things like apostasy, murder, adultery, and the like. Of course, not everyone would commit such sins; many

Christians went their entire lives without needing to have recourse to the sacrament of confession. The sacrament was not viewed as a bandage for Christians who had scraped their knee in a fall, but a life-saving surgery for those who had made a shipwreck of their faith and were in dire need of supernatural intervention lest they perish. Sins less than these were expunged through the penitential acts of every Christian—that is, fasting, almsgiving, and prayer.

Why was the sacrament reserved for such grave cases? As late as the fifth century and the dawn of the Middle Ages, a majority of Christians throughout the West would have been adult converts. As such, they would have received the Sacrament of Baptism upon their conversion. All prior sins would have been dealt with by this sacrament, leaving little occasion for needing confession unless they entirely lapsed in faith later. In other words, a Church composed mainly of converts receiving Baptism as adults had less need for the sacrament of confession.

Public Penance

Another fact about early confession that we may find surprising and uncomfortable is that it was public. A Christian who had fallen away and wanted to repent was expected to confess his fault before the entire congregation in the presence of the bishop and presbyters. There were various reasons for this.

For one thing, Catholics in that time had what we might consider a much more communal approach to things than we do today. It was not sufficient that penitents profess contrition; their contrition needed to be visible to the congregation. Deeds, not words, mattered most. For example, a penitent who came forward and confessed sorrowfully to having lapsed back into paganism could be affirmed by the congregation ("Yes, he is really contrite. He is my neighbor and I have personally witnessed his fasting and almsgiving"), or conversely, his contrition could be contested

("He is not truly contrite! Just yesterday I saw him going to visit the grove of Minerva"). Penitents' contritions were expected to be manifest to the community, not only in their profession of penitence in the midst of the people, but also in the evidence of their penitence demonstrated by daily life under the watchful eye of the community. "Faith apart from works is dead," St. James had written (Jas 2:26); early Christians took this principle to heart when it came to confession.

Presuming penitents were sincere and their contrition was accepted, they would be given a public penance by the bishop. This typically consisted in being assigned to one of the four "orders" of penitents. First there were the *flentes*, the "mourners" and the lowest class of penitents who had committed the worst sins. Their penance was to lay prostrate by the entrance of the church, begging the prayers of those who entered. This sentence usually lasted a year. Then there were the *audientes*, or "hearers." They were allowed to enter the church, stand in the back, and listen to the scriptures and the homily but were required to leave before the Eucharist. They could spend one, two, or even three years at this level. Next came the *substrati*, or "kneelers." These knelt in prayer at the front of the church, were permitted to stay through the prayers, and received the prayers of the bishop but were similarly dismissed before the offering of the Eucharist. Finally, there were the *consistentes*, or "co-standers." These stood with the congregation during the liturgy and were allowed to stay throughout the entire Mass but could not receive Communion. A penitent might be assigned to any of these orders, but whichever he was assigned to, he would be expected to work his way up through each subsequent rank. For example, a notorious sinner might be assigned to begin his penance with the *flentes* but then had to subsequently move up through all the remaining ranks of penitents in a process that could take years. Meanwhile, a less grievous sinner might be assigned to the *consistentes* and readmitted to Communion after only nine months. Only *after* progressing through the orders of penitents would a repentant sinner receive sacramental absolution and return to Communion.

Changing Demographics

This was the state of things at the dawn of the medieval period. Throughout the Dark Ages, however, the sacrament evolved in response to the growth of the Church and changes in society. By the middle of the first millennium, most people in Christendom were born into Christian families and baptized at infancy rather than adulthood. This made it more likely that they would commit various sins after Baptism and that there would be a greater need for confession. Thus, the use of confession began to become more widespread as we move further into the Dark Ages.

We must also note another demographic change in the Church. Most early Christians had come from the Greco-Roman cultural tradition, with its refinement and high civilization, but later generations of Christians were coming from the ranks of the barbarian hordes that were fanning out across Europe. Whereas the Greco-Romans had already possessed civilization, the Germanic barbarians were only coming into civilization at the same time they were embracing Christianity. This means that early Germanic-Catholic culture was a bit more, shall we say, rusticated? So, while two thoughtful Greek-speaking Christians of the late Roman Empire might dialogue eloquently about the theological implications of Arius's theory of *homoiousios*, a Frankish Christian of the Merovingian period had to be reminded that he ought not to commit polygamy and must regrettably refrain from smashing an opponent's head with an ax over a drunken exchange of insults.

Private Confession

The Church quickly realized that if the rigorous ancient disciplines were followed, many people would spend the majority of their lives without being admitted to Communion. As the Middle Ages progressed, the public confession and the orders of penitents were replaced by private confession with penance being administered at the discretion of the confessor. The pioneers of this practice were the Irish missionaries, who compiled penitentials to aid confessors.

The penitential was a book that gave guidance to confessors by discussing particular sins and suggesting various penances for them. An excellent example of an Irish penitential is furnished by the penitential of the monk Cummean, composed around the year 650. Here is an example of some of Cummean's recommendations for confessors:

> One who curses his brother in anger shall make satisfaction to him whom he has cursed and live secluded for seven days on bread and water.
>
> A boy of ten years who steals anything shall do penance for seven days, but if afterward (at the age) of twenty years he happens to commit a small theft, for twenty or forty days.
>
> If anyone, being a gossip, injures the good name of a brother whom he loves, he shall do penance in silence for one or two days.
>
> He who commits theft once shall do penance for one year; if a second time, for two years.[2]

By the eighth century, penitentials had replaced the older forms of the sacrament in most places. The result was that confession transitioned from a public affair carried out in the context of the Christian community into a private affair worked out between the penitent and the confessor.

The Seeds of Indulgences

The transition to individualized penances also corresponded to the rise in what would later be known as indulgences. Indulgences did not begin in the Middle Ages; in fact, they are attested as far back as the third century in the writings of St. Cyprian and Tertullian. *Indulgentia* in Latin means "mercy" or "pardon." Properly understood, an indulgence is a commutation of penance. A sinner might be assigned a penance of two years on bread and water by their confessor. However, if the obligations of their life made such a penance impossible, they might "swap it out" for a different penance—say, making a pilgrimage to a nearby shrine, erecting a chapel, or making a monetary contribution to the Church. This enabled a person to carry out their penance in much briefer time.

Over time these indulgences were equated with days of penance under the old penitentials. For example, going on a pilgrimage to the diocesan cathedral might be equated with forty days penance of bread and water under the old system. This is why books of indulgences right up to the twentieth century might list time designations with each indulgence: "20 days," "7 days," or something similar. Catholics sometimes incorrectly assumed this meant twenty days off purgatory, as if it were a coupon. The reality is that these designations were meant to signify that such and such an indulgence was roughly "worth" twenty days of penance under the old penitentials.

Eucharistic Controversies

It was also the case that even if the Church knew what a sacrament accomplished, it did not necessarily understand *how*. The eucharistic controversies of the ninth to eleventh centuries were an excellent example of how the Church struggled to formulate a vocabulary to explain in what sense Christ was truly present in the Eucharist.

Those unfamiliar with the development of eucharistic theology tend to assume the controversies of the period were over whether Christ was truly present in the Blessed Sacrament. This is incorrect. The early Church had definitively taught that the Blessed Sacrament was truly the Body and Blood of Christ, a consensus that passed on into medieval Christianity as an essential part of belief in both the East and the West. Early medieval Catholics were thus in broad agreement that Christ was truly present in the Blessed Sacrament. What they disputed was the *manner* in which he was present and how this related to the sacramental species of bread and wine.

The debate dated back to the mid-ninth century and the reign of the Carolingian Charles the Bald. It began with a book entitled *De Corpore et Sanguine Domine* written by the learned French monk, St. Paschasius Radbertus. St. Paschasius had undertaken to explain the true doctrine of the Eucharist based on the teaching of the Fathers and the saints. In his work, Paschasius drew heavily on writings from the saints—especially Ambrose, Augustine, and Chrysostom—and provided a thorough exegesis of John 6 and 1 Corinthians 11, which are the most heavily eucharistic passages of the New Testament. These he seasoned with accounts of eucharistic miracles to make his point that in the Eucharist we have nothing other than the real, historic Body of Christ itself, the same Body that was born of the Virgin, suffered on the Cross, and was resurrected. The book was presented to Emperor Charles the Bald in 844.

Without getting bogged down in the nuances of St. Paschasius's doctrine (in some points he identifies Christ's sacramental presence too closely with his natural body), it suffices to say that the book aroused some opposition in the Church. When Emperor Charles became aware of the controversy, he asked another respected ecclesiastic, Ratramnus of Corbie, to write a rebuttal. Ratramnus insisted that Christ's body was truly present in the Eucharist, but only in a spiritual manner, and as such the eucharistic Body is not the same body that was born of Mary, suffered, and was resurrected. We might term this the "spiritual" view as opposed to St. Paschasius's "carnal" view.

Leading ecclesiastics and theologians each took sides; famed theologians Rabanus Maurus, Walafrid Strabo, Christian Druthmar, and Florus Magister all supported the view of Ratramnus, while the influential Hincmar of Reims and Haimo of Halberstadt supported St. Paschasius. In general, St. Paschasius seems to have been supported more by the bishops; Ratramnus, by the theologians.

The leading supporter of the "spiritual" view of Ratramnus was none other than the eminent theologian and Neoplatonist philosopher John Scotus Eriugena. No doubt influenced by Platonic theories of forms and ideas, Eriugena had supported the notion that what is received at the Eucharist are forms or "figures" of Christ. (The contemporary Hincmar of Reims says this assertion was among Eriugena's greatest errors.) Eriugena's support of Ratramnus lent his theory great weight, but St. Paschasius perhaps had even a weightier supporter in Pope Sylvester II (999–1003), who with the Roman Church believed and taught a miraculous transformation of the elements at the priestly consecration. Sylvester was so invested in that he wrote a treatise defending the interpretation of St. Paschasius.

The controversy was not effectively resolved in the ninth century, primarily because of the Viking invasions. Paris was attacked the very year after St. Paschasius presented his treatise to Charles the Bald, which of course meant the emperor had more pressing matters to attend to. The subsequent weakening and extinction of the Carolingian monarchy brought an end to the scholarly theological debates among monks that had characterized the Carolingian Renaissance. But though the debate ended, it was never really settled. French ecclesiastics and theologians continued to maintain their own distinctive opinions on the matter.

Up Close and Personal:
ST. PASCHASIUS RADBERTUS

One of the most important figures in the Carolingian eucharistic controversy was St. Paschasius Radbertus (ca. 786–860). As an infant, St. Paschasius was abandoned by his family and left on the steps of the convent of Notre-Dame de Soissons. He was raised by the nuns there and through the convent became acquainted with some very holy role models, including the abbess Theodrara and her two brothers, Adalard and Wala, both monks at the monastery of Corbie.

When he came of age, Paschasius himself entered Corbie, eventually becoming abbot. St. Paschasius eventually resigned the abbacy to devote himself to study and spiritual writing, and it was during this period that he composed his famous treatise on the Body of Christ that would be the catalyst for the Carolingian eucharistic controversy. He lived a long and fruitful life and died around the age of seventy-four, an exceptionally old age for the time. He was initially buried in the church of St. John at Corbie, but when numerous miracles were reported at his grave, his remains were solemnly removed by order of Pope St. Gregory VII in 1073 and reburied in the church of St. Peter in Corbie. His feast is on April 26.

Not Whether, but How

Despite the variety of opinions on the matter, it is important to note that the Carolingian eucharistic controversy was not over whether the Church taught that Christ is present in the Eucharist. Both sides, St. Paschasius and Ratramnus and their supporters and detractors, all believed in the "real presence" of Christ, but they debated the meaning of the term *real* and in what nature Christ was truly present. St. Paschasius seemed to understand this in an extremely carnal sense—that what the believer is consuming is not the substance of Christ's body but both the substance and accidents that only a miracle prevents us from seeing. Of course, in the ninth century theologians had not yet appropriated the vocabulary of *substance* and *accidents* in reference to the Eucharist, which made the discussion even more muddled.

Ratramnus seemed to sense the inherent problem with Paschasius's opinion and posited a spiritual presence instead, akin to the way the Holy Spirit is present in a believer's soul, but in a more profound way. It was a true presence, but in a different mode than the carnal interpretation put forth by St. Paschasius. In other words, both sides agreed in a "real presence"; neither side taught that Communion was purely symbolic.

Inadequate Explanations

Essentially, the Carolingian eucharistic controversy was the Church's first attempt to work out the distinctions between sacramental form and matter, as well as the more important distinctions between Christ's *modes* of presence. St. Paschasius knew the presence of Christ was real in a sense that was more than just a spiritual mode. Ratramnus, however, rightly suspected that Christ's real presence should not be understood in a carnal sense, which seemed to be the extreme that St. Paschasius was suggesting. This suspicion caused Ratramnus to wrongly deny any change in the elements of bread and wine. What both theologians were looking for was a thoroughly worked-out doctrine of a *sacramental mode* of presence, as opposed to one that was merely spiritual or merely carnal.

We come now to the most familiar name associated with this controversy, that of Berengar of Tours. A monk of Tours and celebrated teacher, Berengar's famous denial of a substantial change in the eucharistic elements caused a rift in the eleventh-century Church that would lead to thirty years of contention and culminate in deeply significant developments in sacramental theology on a level not seen since the patristic period.

The Berengar controversy looks back and forward; on the one hand, the response of the Church of his day to his heresy clearly shows that the

Church always understood Christ to be truly present in the Sacrament of the Eucharist. On the other hand, the questions and problems posed by Berengar led to many important developments in theology, especially the adoption of the term *transubstantiation* to describe the change in the elements and the manner of Christ's presence.

Berengar's Heresy

Berengar was born sometime around 999 in the city of Tours. It is unknown whether his origins were humble or noble. Tours had been a very important ecclesiastical center ever since it was graced by the presence of St. Martin in the fourth century and Gregory of Tours in the sixth. During the time of Charlemagne it became the center of the Carolingian Renaissance due to Alcuin, the famous monk-scribe who was abbot of Marmoutier Abbey in Tours. The city was also the capital of the province of Touraine from the ninth century on, so that by the time Berengar was born, Tours was an important political and ecclesiastical hub, populated by some of the most creative political and religious thinkers of the high Middle Ages. It was an atmosphere ripe for intellectual inquiry.

Berengar completed primary studies in Tours and then went on to the cathedral school at Chartres where he studied under the famous Fulbert, bishop of Chartres. Berengar was distinguished by his quick thought and penetrating intellect, though he does not always seem to have been in agreement with Fulbert, who disapproved of Berengar's independent streak. After his higher education was completed, Berengar took over the famous school of St. Martin at Tours and earned a reputation throughout the Church as a gifted teacher and brilliant theologian. He was appointed archdeacon of Angers in 1037 but was allowed to continue teaching at Tours. Popular, erudite, and demonstrating a penetrating theological insight mixed with a bit of cutting-edge speculation and a disposition toward rationalism, Berengar was the celebrity theologian of the eleventh century.

As sometimes happens with celebrities, Berengar's opinions eventually got him into trouble. As we have seen, prior to Berengar there had been a lively debate going on in France over the manner in which Christ was present in the Holy Eucharist. Berengar would ultimately assert that the presence of Christ in the Eucharist was merely spiritual and not physical in any sense, a teaching that would erupt into the biggest controversy in the French church of the eleventh century.

It was at the St. Martin School of Tours that Berengar apparently began teaching the doctrine of Ratramnus: that the Eucharist was endowed with a purely spiritual presence of Christ without a substantial change in the elements of bread and wine. As the dispute of the ninth century had never been really settled, the teaching of Berengar began attracting attention from other theologians who opposed it. This led to the examination of Berengar's teaching by two prelates, Hugues, bishop of Langres, and Adelman, bishop of Liège. The two bishops apparently could not come to an agreement on the orthodoxy of Berengar's teaching, which itself testifies to the imprecise nature of sacramental theology at the time. Adelman appealed to the authority of John Scotus Eriugena in support of Berengar while Hugues dissented.

But at this point a more eminent ecclesiastic was drawn into the debate, Lanfranc of Bec, who was at that time the well-regarded abbot of Bec monastery in Normandy. Lanfranc combined saintliness and erudition in a manner that prefigured Aquinas, and his school at Bec was one of the most renowned in all Christendom. Hearing Berengar supported by an appeal to Eriugena, Lanfranc condemned Eriugena's opinion as heretical and espoused the doctrine of real change in the elements as put forward by St. Paschasius. The debate of the ninth century was suddenly reopened.

Debate and Division

Around this time (1050), Berengar's teaching was beginning to divide the Church regionally. Sensing a bigger problem brewing, a conference of local bishops summoned Berengar to appear before inquiries at Brionne and Chartres. The records of these proceedings are lost; it seems Berengar appeared in person to defend his doctrine but was unsuccessful.

During Easter of 1050, Lanfranc went on a journey to Rome to participate in a local council of the Roman Church. This council was not connected with Berengar initially; it had to do with trying charges of simony and other matters connected with the burgeoning Gregorian Reform movement. This council was extremely well attended, and with fifty-five bishops and thirty-two abbots present, Lanfranc brought the matter of Berengar to the attention of Pope Leo IX and the council. Berengar's teaching was soundly condemned by the council, and Pope Leo ordered him to appear before a regional council at Vercelli the same year to answer charges of heresy.

At this time, for reasons not entirely clear, the French king Henri I denied Berengar permission to attend this Council of Vercelli and instead had him imprisoned. The Council of Vercelli convened in September 1050 and examined Berengar's doctrine *in absentia*. The spiritual view was there condemned as heresy. At this point Berengar's teaching on the Eucharist had been condemned four times: at Brionne, Chartres, Rome, and Vercelli.

Surprisingly, Berengar's condemnations did not detract from his broad base of support. One of the most eminent theologians in favor of Berengar was Eusebius Bruno, Berengar's disciple and the bishop of Angers. The powerful count of Anjou, Geoffrey II, also supported him. It was not immediately apparent, after all, that the controversy was settled. Ratramnus, Eriugena, and their supporters had been in good standing with the Church during the Carolingian eucharistic controversy, and at first it was not clearly perceived why Berengar's opinions could not likewise be tolerated. But the Church of the eleventh century was not the Church of the ninth, and while sacramental theology was still in a very formative stage in Ratramnus's day, by the time of Berengar it had been developed with much more precision, making Berengar's teachings more outside the pale of orthodoxy.

Berengar was condemned a fifth time by a regional synod summoned by the king in 1054. After this, Berengar appears to have repented. He signed formulas of faith at the Council of Tours (1055) and Rome (1059) affirming that after the consecration, the "real and sensible" Body and Blood of Christ are present in the Holy Eucharist.

The remainder of Berengar's life is a sad tale. Berengar would go back on his oaths and attack the formulary of Rome, which caused much of his support to evaporate, including that of his friend and disciple, Eusebius Bruno. His doctrine would be condemned so soundly and repeatedly that it would be impossible to state that the Church's stance this point was ambiguous; he was condemned in 1075, 1076, 1078, and 1080. Ratramnus's book was also condemned during the controversy and would later be put on the Index of Forbidden Books.

Berengar finally signed a very explicit profession of faith in 1080, was reconciled with the Church, and spent the last eight years of his life doing penance on the island of St. Cosme, home to a small priory in the midst of the Loire River outside of the city. There he died in union with the Church in 1088.

Theology and Tradition

There are several things we can observe concerning the heresy of Berengar. First, it is interesting to note that, throughout the dispute, most of those who supported Berengar were secular princes (like the count of Anjou) and lesser theologians. His opposition came mainly from bishops and the hierarchy, and the most eminent theologians of the day (Lanfranc, for example) were unanimous in their condemnation of Berengar. No great theologian of the age supported him. As in the case with St. Paschasius and Ratramnus, the secularists and middling theologians stood on the side of dissent while it fell to the pope and bishops, no doubt guided by the "sure charism of truth" (*CCC*, 94) that the bishops possess collectively in union with the pope, to state the truth clearly.

It is from the standpoint of eucharistic apologetics, however, that the controversy of Berengar's teaching really becomes apparent. Anti-Catholic writers typically state that belief in transubstantiation was invented at the Fourth Lateran Council (1215), or will at least suggest that the eleventh century was the time when the Church first started teaching a change in the elements. The Berengar controversy blows away these assertions. As we have seen, Berengar was merely adding his two cents in a controversy that went back to the mid-ninth century. The ninth-century dispute between St. Paschasius and Ratramnus was not over the introduction of a novelty into the Church's theology. Both Paschasius and Ratramnus accepted that Christ was "really present" in the Eucharist but debated what manner of presence this was.

A tradition had been handed on from the patristic age that the Sacrament of the Eucharist is the Body and Blood of Christ. Christians, without interruption from the time of the Fathers onward, held that the manner in which Christ was present in the sacrament was a real presence. The point is nobody ever doubted the real presence, and the heresy of Berengar did not constitute a denial of the real presence in the strict sense. Berengar sought to explain the manner in which the real presence was confected, just as Ratramnus did before him. The fact that Berengar did not accept the concept of a substantial change in the elements at the time of consecration is no evidence that the Church at his time or before did not believe in the real presence. Nobody ever seriously doubted the real presence, even if they did question the manner in which that presence became real—was it truly miraculous, or was it a spiritual transformation that, while supernatural, was not necessarily a miracle?

The Golden Thread of Orthodoxy

As the Roman liturgy developed in the early Middle Ages, the consecration came to be regarded as the focal point of the eucharistic mystery. This is the historical explanation for the Western Church's emphasis on the consecration over the epiclesis as the moment when the Body of Christ becomes present. The subsequent developments in sacramental theology (including the institution of the Feast of Corpus Christi, the addition of the elevation of the host after consecration, and the adoption of the term *transubstantiation* in the mid-twelfth century) and the emerging distinctions of a sacramental mode of presence show that Berengar stood outside the direction that the Church's theology had been developing. Ironically, the term *transubstantiation* was first coined by Hildebert of Lavardin, believed to be a onetime disciple of Berengar.

There is a principle of development, expounded by St. John Henry Newman in his *Essay on the Development of Doctrine*, that earlier Catholic teachings can be more clearly understood in light of subsequent developments. Using this principle, we see that the teachings of Ratramnus, Eriugena, and Berengar on the "spiritual" presence of Christ in the Eucharist without a substantial change in the elements were outside the bounds of orthodoxy even in their own day. This is why men like St. Paschasius and Lanfranc of Bec, as well as the papacy itself, responded so vehemently against Berengar's hypotheses.

Eucharistic doctrine might not have been perfectly worked out in the eleventh century, but when faced with Berengar's adamant denial of a physical presence of Christ, the Church knew something was wrong. And thus his teaching was unanimously condemned eight times during his life and even once after his death (1095). These facts do not make any sense if the Church was the one innovating with the insistence of a change in substance, but they do make perfect sense if Berengar was the one teaching novelty. It is a classic case of doctrine in a state of development, demonstrating how earlier teachings can be interpreted in light of later developments to identify the golden thread of orthodoxy that runs through the Church's teaching in all ages.

On the positive side, the Church defines only what is disputed. Berengar's heresy led to a further development of the concepts of what medieval theologians would describe as the *sacramentum tantum* (sacramental sign) and the *sacramentum et res* (the mystical reality), as well as the further crystallization of the concepts of form, matter, and accidental properties in the eucharistic species.

Perhaps most importantly, the controversy led the way to understanding the concept of Christ's *sacramental* mode of presence in the Eucharist. This sacramental mode of being is more specific and particular than the omnipresence of the Word in all places and times throughout the universe, which is predicated on the fact that God is a pure spirit and is eternal in power. Nevertheless, it is different from his physical, historic presence on the earth, because those who encounter Christ in the sacrament encounter him in a real way, but not in a carnal way. We truly receive the Body, Blood, Soul, and Divinity of Christ, but not in a carnal sense in which we are cannibals gnawing on bone marrow.

St. Paschasius had known from tradition that Christ is truly and really present, but he lacked the vocabulary or the specificity to distinguish Christ's real presence from his fleshly, historic existence on the earth, which is why many who read his treatise found something awry in it. The sacramental mode of presence that was elucidated by theologians after Berengar helped explain how the Church could at once affirm Christ's true, substantial presence in the Eucharist in a special way different from his omnipresence while at the same time denying that Christ is present in a carnal manner in the Eucharist.

We can also deduce in the heresy of Berengar an emergence of the rationalist trend that would eventually sour the latter Scholastic period. Though there is nothing known for certain, contemporaries of Berengar mentioned that he also denied the extent of the Church's spiritual power, the legitimacy of infant Baptism, and the indissolubility of marriage. While we do not know how well formed these theses were, they do demonstrate a trend in Berengar's thought toward denying the objective spiritual realities brought about by the sacraments (objective baptismal regeneration, the bond of matrimony, and so on)—what later theologians would call the *ex opera operato* manner in which the sacraments produce their effects. This rationalist critique of the objective nature of the sacraments would reappear in the fourteenth century and come to a head with Luther's insistence that faith alone (understood entirely subjectively) is the operative principle behind any effect wrought by grace.

Thus, though the heresy of Berengar split the French church during the eleventh century, it was the occasion of great developments in medieval sacramental theology that would culminate in the theology of Peter Lombard and Thomas Aquinas in the twelfth and thirteenth centuries.

By the year 1000, the sacramental practice of the Church looked a lot more like what we would recognize today. But the Church was also developing in other ways. Next, we will learn how a group of pious monks started a movement for the moral reform of the clergy.

YOU BE THE JUDGE:

Is the dogma of the real presence of Christ in the Eucharist a late medieval invention?

A cursory search of Protestant apologetics on the Eucharist will reveal an oft-repeated claim that the Catholic teaching of transubstantiation was invented at the Fourth Lateran Council in

1215. It is true that the council defined this doctrine, but does that mean transubstantiation was invented in 1215? Certainly not.

The transformation of the bread and wine into the Body and Blood of Christ in the Mass had been taught all the way back to apostolic times. St. Ignatius of Antioch, writing around the year 110, warned of certain heretics who "do not confess that the Eucharist is the flesh of our Savior Jesus Christ, flesh which suffered for our sins and which that Father, in his goodness, raised up again. They who deny the gift of God are perishing in their disputes."[3] Berengar in the eleventh century is the first person we know of to ever explicitly and formally deny the real presence. The Fourth Lateran Council in 1215 did not invent the teaching of transubstantiation but merely coined the use of the word *transubstantiation* to describe the miraculous change in the elements that occurs at Mass—a tenet of faith the Church had always held and taught.

Chapter 10

The Cluniac Reform

One of the delicious ironies of God's providence is how he sometimes uses the very means employed to oppress his people in order to deliver them. Goliath was decapitated by his own sword, and the wicked man who digs a pit for his enemy falls into it himself, as the psalmist says. Similarly, it was a layman who set in motion the chain of events that would ultimately undermine lay domination of the Church. We can begin this fascinating story here, but we must wait until the appropriate period of Church history (and the next volume of the series) to witness its conclusion.

We have already cataloged the various ways an enterprising lay prince might control the Church in his domain (see chapter 8). One popular method was by the founding of a monastery, whose abbot would be chosen by the lord. Management of the abbey's funds would then be farmed out to a lay administrator in the service of the lord. This system enabled the local noble to exert control over a monastery through its abbot while giving him access to its revenues through his administrator. And such was the state of things for many years throughout much of Latin Christendom.

But in the year 893, a certain count named William from Auvergne, in France, made war on the neighboring duchy of Aquitaine and conquered it, taking the title William I, duke of Aquitaine. William was a very devout man, so much so that his countrymen called him "William the Pious." He founded numerous monastic houses around Aquitaine throughout his reign (893–918), but by far the most important was that of Cluny, founded in 910.

The land William deeded over to the monks of Cluny included vineyards, woodlands, fields, rivers, mills, serfs, and all manner of lands, both cultivated and uncultivated—everything a monastery needed to be self-sufficient. In addition to praying the Divine Office, the monks of Cluny were to extend hospitality to pilgrims, travelers, and the poor. But the most unique part of Cluny's deed was its stipulation that the monastery be entirely free from the interference of local authorities, whether ecclesiastical or lay, including William himself. The monastery was, in theory, subject only to the pope, although even he could not meddle in the monks' affairs without their consent. To underscore the sincerity of his wishes, William entrusted the monastery to the patronage of Sts. Peter and Paul and placed a solemn curse on anyone who should dare violate its charter.

Why would a layman like William confer such a radical degree of independence on a monastery? Though a powerful lord who could have done whatever he liked, William was a devoted Catholic and desired the good of the Church. He knew he had no business meddling in the internal affairs of a monastery and wanted the monks to be free to serve God in whatever way they thought best.

The result of this was that the monastery of Cluny enjoyed a degree of independence unique in Latin Christendom. Cluny's first abbot, St. Berno, was chosen by William specifically because of his reputation as a zealous, reform-minded monk who desired to elevate the spiritual life of the Benedictines. Together, St. Berno and William envisioned Cluny as an enclosed garden where the flowers of holiness could grow unmolested by worldly interlopers of any kind.

Up Close and Personal:
ST. BERNO

St. Berno was the first abbot of Cluny, serving from 909 until 925. He was the progenitor of the Cluniac reforms that later came to characterize Benedictine monasticism in the tenth and eleventh centuries. Berno was born into the Burgundian nobility around 850. As a young man he witnessed his father open his estates to the Benedictines of Glanfueil Abbey, who were fleeing the Viking raids.

Berno was inspired to join the Benedictines and was professed at the Abbey of St. Martin of Autun. Even as a young monk, Berno was devoted to a stricter application of the Rule of St. Benedict and earned a reputation as a pious, honest monk of the burgeoning reform movement. With his own resources he founded the monastery of St. Peter of Gigny, dedicated to prayer, silence, and solitude. This pious work had the support of the pope and the king of Burgundy. Another like monastery was founded at Baume shortly afterward.

By then Berno had established such a reputation that Duke William of Aquitaine entrusted him with two more monasteries, at Deols and Massay. With these monasteries successfully reformed, William approached Berno with the project for which both would be remembered throughout the annals of ecclesiastical history: the foundation of Cluny. A famous tale tells us that when Duke William asked Berno where the new monastery should be built, Berno asked the duke to donate his favorite hunting lodge. The duke was put out and replied, "Impossible. I cannot have my dogs removed." St. Berno replied, "Drive out the dogs and put monks in their place, for thou can well think what reward God will give you for dogs, and what for monks."[1] Duke William accordingly gave up the land, and Cluny was founded. Berno died in 927 and was venerated as a saint soon after. His feast day is January 13.

Monasteries in Crisis

Before we discuss the reforms that sprung from Cluny, we must pause and consider the state of monasticism in the tenth century to understand why St. Berno and those like him believed reform was necessary.

Monastic life in tenth-century Europe was in trouble, for various reasons. From the eighth century on, western Europe had suffered from almost continuous Viking raids. Viking marauders used Europe's network of rivers to reach far into the interior, sacking monasteries and towns. Sometimes, they carved out entire swaths of territory for themselves—as the Norse did when they settled in Normandy the year after the foundation of Cluny. The constant pillaging destabilized society and made it difficult for monasteries to attain the kind of unperturbed self-sufficiency originally envisioned by St. Benedict. Monastic life became irregular, and in many places discipline broke down entirely.

Furthermore, as we have noted elsewhere, lay pilfering of monastic revenues meant that many monasteries existed on the margins of poverty, which undermined the material stability St. Benedict believed a monastery ought to enjoy. These impoverished abbeys attracted few novices and were often places where monastic discipline was difficult to maintain.

By contrast, some feudal lords founded monasteries with the intention of retiring to them some day. These monasteries, as the prospective nursing home of the local noble, were funded lavishly and in accordance with the taste of their patron. The Rule of St. Benedict was modified to suit the tastes of the retired lord. For example, Matins might be moved so it would not interfere with the lord's sleep, or the vegetarian diet expanded for the lord's benefit. In these monasteries, monks wore richer, warmer clothing and were permitted to disregard the monastic customs of fasting. Such practices were hardly in keeping with the spirit (or text!) of the Benedictine Rule.

Ongoing Reform

William and St. Berno were very cognizant of these problems and seemed to have believed they could be remedied by a more independent abbot, and thus was Cluny established free from any local jurisdiction. Berno used this independence to create a monastic regimen at Cluny whose fidelity to the Rule of St. Benedict became the envy of the Benedictine Order. Cluny's reputation spread, and before long devout souls from all over France were coming to join St. Berno's congregation. The numbers swelled such that Berno had to found additional monasteries to take in all the novices. By the time of St. Berno's death in 927, Cluny had blossomed into a congregation with six daughter houses.

The work of reform was carried on by Berno's successor, St. Odo of Cluny, who served as abbot from 927 until his death in 942. Cluny expanded significantly under Odo, receiving several grants of land and other gifts. The abbey became the jewel of all the abbeys in France, renowned for the size of its congregation, the security of its endowments, and the regularity of its monastic life. Other monks began to covet the abbacy of Cluny. On one occasion, a hostile monk from another monastery attempted to gain control of Cluny. Only the personal intervention of Pope John X and King Rudolf of France secured the abbacy for Odo.

Such was the reputation of St. Odo and Cluny that Odo was not only confirmed in his position by the pope but also given special authority to reform other monasteries. The work of reform was often met with fierce resistance. Many French monasteries had been in disarray for a long time and had no desire to return to strict observance of Benedict's rule. The monks of such monasteries bitterly opposed St. Odo's authority.

For example, in 930 St. Odo attempted to reform Fleury Abbey, near Orleans on the Loire. Founded in 640, Fleury was famous as the final resting place of the bones of St. Benedict himself. But in Odo's day Fleury was in bad shape. Continuous Viking raids had caused the monks to temporarily abandon Fleury on several occasions. The disruptions led to a lapse in the observation of the rule, such that the monks had gotten accustomed to a life of leisure. When they heard St. Odo had been sent to reform them, they met him on the road armed with spears and swords threatening to kill him. Odo was only admitted to the monastery after a three-day standoff.

Nevertheless, the work of reform continued, with Odo traveling as far abroad as Aquitaine and Italy in his work. Many reformed monasteries would go on to reform other monasteries. The Cluniac observance became the monastic standard of the West for more than a century.

Influence of the Cluny Ideal

The spread of the Cluniac observance saw the diffusion of Cluniac ideals. While the heart of the Cluniac vision was simply a return to the strict observance of the Rule of St. Benedict, the Cluniac reform came to be associated with several other ideas as well: splendid liturgies, polyphonic music, and a monastic life more intensively focused on silence and contemplation.

Widespread, these ideals had consequences both positive and negative. On the one hand, the focus on prayer and liturgy reinvigorated the spiritual life of the monasteries. It even spilled out into the lay world, with the emergence of devotions such as "Our Lady's Psalter," essentially the Rosary in a very raw form. The monks became more socially conscious, supporting two initiatives called the "Peace of God" and "Truce of God." These were the first large-scale peace movements in European history. They attempted to civilize warfare by prohibiting attacks on clergy and noncombatants, restricting the occasions upon which nobles could fight one another, and exempting church property from physical violence. The devotion of the Cluniacs nudged the society in a direction more pious and humane.

On the other hand, the new emphasis on extravagant liturgy meant that monks devoted less time to manual labor. The result was the emergence of the "choir monk," religious who devoted all of their time to the Divine Office and private contemplation. Manual labor, then, was relegated to servants called lay brothers, men who partook to some degree in the monastic life but did not participate in singing the Divine Office. The task of the lay brother was to see to the temporal needs of the monastery, laboring on behalf of the choir monks.

Often this division was one of class—the choir monks were the sons of the nobility while the lay brothers were commoners, and often illiterate. Later religious orders such as the Cistercians and Carthusians would formalize this arrangement, designating the lay brothers by the name *conversi* and formally absolving the choir monks of all manual labor. The surgical excision of manual labor from the life of the average monk and introduction of class distinction into the very halls of the monastery is a far cry from St. Benedict's *ora et labora* and surely one of the most regrettable developments of the Middle Ages.

Cleaning Up Corruption

In all this we see that the organizing principle of Cluny was *independence*—the idea that a monastery was best governed when it was independent of lay control, or that monks should be able to focus exclusively on prayer through independence from manual labor, or that the Church should enjoy a measure of independence from the violence of warring nobility. Indeed, the Cluniac ideal was nothing other than the independence of the Church from all that dragged it down, mired it in grime, and obscured its divine mission.

Hence, as Cluniac ideals spread, monastic reformers clamored for an end to the abuses that were endemic throughout the Church. Simony— the buying and selling of Church offices—was particularly odious. The scandal reached right up to the papacy. In 1032, Benedict IX was elected pope by open bribery. And such things were happening up and down the entire hierarchy.

Clerical concubinage was another grave problem. The ideal since the earliest days of Christianity had been for clerics in major orders to live celibate. It is true that some clerics in the early centuries were married, but these married clergy (in the Latin rite, at least) were often expected to live in a state of sexual continence with their wives.[2] By the end of the first millennium, however, the discipline was irregularly observed. It was not uncommon for bishops and priests to keep mistresses publicly, to the great scandal of the faithful. A call to return to the ideals of clerical celibacy was another force that came out of the Cluniac reform.

Ending Lay Domination

Important though these issues were, the burgeoning energy of this movement would ultimately coalesce into a single beam directed against one principal problem: lay domination of the Church. As we have seen, the Church of the first millennium suffered under the influence of powerful laypersons in a variety of ways. The emblem of this lay domination was the practice of lay investiture, the ceremony whereby a bishop-elect did homage to a lay lord, who presented him with the signs of his office (the episcopal staff and ring). As the Church crossed the threshold of the first millennium, the movement against lay domination increasingly became a crusade to end lay investiture.

It was in this atmosphere that one of the most remarkable men in the history of the Church arose: the monk Hildebrand. Not much is known of Hildebrand's origins; he was born in Tuscany of humble parentage sometime in the 1020s. His family sent him to be educated at the Santa Maria monastery on the Aventine hill in Rome, where his uncle was abbot. Santa Maria had adopted the Cluniac reform some years prior, and Cluniac ideals pervaded the cloister. It was thus at Santa Maria that young Hildebrand was first exposed to the austere principles of the reform that would characterize his entire ecclesiastical career. Hildebrand took vows as a

Benedictine in Rome and entered the service of John Gratian, the notable archpriest of San Giovanni by the Latin Gate. Shortly thereafter, this Gratian was elevated to the papacy as Pope Gregory VI, taking Hildebrand with him to be papal chaplain.

The pontificate of Gregory VI (1045–1046) was brief and troubled. The prior pontiff, Benedict IX, was a scandalous pope who resigned the papacy so he could marry his lover. Gregory VI was elected in wake of the resignation. But a faction of the Roman nobility had already acclaimed a rival pope, Sylvester III, and seized a portion of the city of Rome. To make matters worse, Benedict IX was unable to marry the woman for whom he had resigned and immediately attempted to withdraw his resignation. He, too, seized a portion of the city and fortified it. There were now three claimants to the See of Peter.

The chaos in Rome necessitated the intervention of the Holy Roman emperor. Henry III of Germany accordingly marched into Rome in 1046 and presided over the Synod of Sutri, which was meant to settle the dispute of the three popes. Gregory VI was recognized as the valid pope but lacked the support of the bishops to govern effectively. Lingering accusations of simony compelled Gregory to resign, and he went to Cologne in exile, accompanied by Hildebrand, his faithful chaplain. When Gregory died in 1048, Hildebrand traveled to France to spend a year at Cluny.

In 1049 Hildebrand made another fortuitous acquaintance, that of Bruno of Toul who had recently been elected Pope Leo IX and was en route to Rome to be installed. The pope-elect took on Hildebrand, made him a cardinal-subdeacon, and appointed him administrator of the Patrimony of St. Peter. Here Hildebrand exhibited an exceptional capacity for administration that made him an invaluable asset to the papal court. Leo IX died in 1054, but Hildebrand continued his work in the court through six more popes, eventually becoming a "kingmaker" among the cardinals capable of supporting a candidate all the way to the chair of St. Peter. All the while, he pushed the Cluniac agenda by reforming monasteries, promoting the moral reform of the clergy, and pushing back against lay investiture.

In 1073, Hildebrand was elected pope by acclamation and took the name Gregory VII. By the time Hildebrand became pope, he was known all over Christendom as the most zealous promoter of the Cluniac reforms. Now, with the chief reformer sitting on the chair of St. Peter, the fight against lay investiture was about to escalate drastically.

And it is here that we must leave the illustrious career of this gifted man, for we have now moved out of the Dark Ages and into the High Middle Ages, the subject of the next book in this series. Next, we shall draw some concluding observations about the development of the Church throughout the Dark Ages before bidding farewell to this extraordinary millennium.

YOU BE THE JUDGE:

Was priestly celibacy an innovation of the late Middle Ages?

Clerical celibacy is not a doctrine of the Church. Rather, it is a discipline, a long-standing practice of the Church that, *in theory*, could be changed—something people continue to argue about to this day. When evaluating an ecclesiastical discipline, we must understand how old it is. Some disciplines are extremely ancient, such as the forty-day fast of Lent, or the necessity of attending Mass on Sundays and holy days. Such disciplines are so intimately connected with various aspects of the faith that getting rid of them could have tremendous consequences. When it comes to clerical celibacy, opponents of the discipline often argue that it dates from "only" the Middle Ages and hence is "not really that ancient."

So how old is the discipline of clerical celibacy in the West? Those who point to a medieval origin for clerical celibacy are usually referring to the period of the Cluniac and Gregorian Reforms (910–1080). During this period, reformers such as St. Odo, St. Peter Damian, and Pope St. Gregory VII advocated for a stricter observance of clerical celibacy. They encouraged clerics to honor the custom of celibacy and put away their mistresses, if they had them. By the second millennium, the tradition of celibacy had become more institutionalized than before.

But we ought not to confuse the medieval promotion of clerical celibacy with a medieval origin for the discipline. In fact, the discipline goes all the way back to apostolic times. The confusion is due to the fact that, even if the early Church frequently featured married priests, the priests were expected to remain sexually continent. That is to say, even if we can point to the Cluniac and Gregorian reforms as a time when celibacy was highly emphasized, clerics had *always* been expected to remain sexually continent from the earliest days of the Church—married or not.

For example, the Church Father Origen (ca. 220) wrote that a priest who offered the Holy Sacrifice of the Mass could not also be sexually active:

> I will express what the words of the Apostle mean, but I am afraid that some will be saddened. Do not refuse yourselves to each other, unless through a mutual agreement for a given occasion, so as to free yourselves for prayer, and then come together again; it is therefore certain that perpetual sacrifice is impossible for those who are subject to the obligations of marriage. . . . I therefore conclude that only the one vowed to perpetual chastity can offer the perpetual sacrifice.[3]

And the thirty-third canon of the Council of Elvira (305) said:

> It has seemed good to absolutely forbid the bishops, the
> priests, and the deacons, i.e., all the clerics in the service
> of the sacred ministry, to have relations with their wives
> and procreate children; should anyone do so, let him be
> excluded from the honor of the clergy.[4]

Many such statements can be found in the writings of Tertullian,
Eusebius, and other early Church Fathers. The impression we
are left with is that the Church always expected its clerics to be
sexually abstinent, whether they were married or not. The chaos
of the Dark Ages made it difficult to maintain this discipline, and
abuses crept in. What the Cluniac and Gregorian reformers did
was not so much propose a new discipline but rather insist on a
return to an ancient one.

Conclusion

Transformation and Continuity

Writing a history of the so-called Dark Ages is inherently challenging because of the period's transitional nature. As such, any line drawn as the end of this era—such as the Truce of God in 1027—is bound to be a bit arbitrary. The Dark Ages followed closely upon the demise of the Western Roman Empire and were in turn followed by the High Middle Ages. Throughout the centuries covered in this book we can see the Dark Ages either emerging from the former or transforming into the latter. It can be difficult to see the Dark Ages for what they were rather than what they came from or led to.

This difficulty becomes more acute when we try to specifically shed light on the Catholic Church in the Dark Ages. Like society at large, the Church in the period was undergoing a tremendous transformation. It's astonishing to think about the different worlds inhabited by saints at each end of the chronological spectrum, between, say, St. Augustine of Hippo and St. Odo of Cluny. The ground had completely shifted under the Church during these tumultuous centuries. While the Church of Roman times was part of a shared political and cultural heritage, the Church of the Dark Ages was diffused across cultures and political systems of incredible diversity—the clans of Ireland, the urbanized society of northern Italy, and the hardy Visigoths spreading out across the tablelands of Hispania. Thus the story of the Church in the Dark Ages is largely the story of how the Church, ever guided by the Holy Spirit, responded to these changes.

Indeed, the great thread of continuity throughout this period was the doctrine of the Church. Though the Roman world had collapsed, the monks and theologians of the early Middle Ages continued to drink deeply from the font of patristic authors such as St. Augustine and St. Jerome, taking the greatest thought of the early Church and planting it in medieval soil. There is a marvelous chain of continuity between the late patristic Fathers and the luminaries of the eighth and ninth centuries, with monumental characters such as St. Benedict or Pope St. Gregory the Great bridging the gap between the ancient and medieval epochs. This is not to say theological development did not happen; it surely did, as we saw especially with regard to the sacraments. But the development flowed seamlessly and organically from the tradition that preceded it, as all authentic Catholic development does.

The liturgy, too, provided a concrete source of unity for the Church throughout the centuries. In the early Middle Ages, what we would refer to today as the "Latin rite" consisted of a variety of localized usages sharing the same essential structure and use of the Latin language. By the eighth century the dominant variant of the Latin rite was that practiced in the Church of Rome. The dominance of the Roman liturgy was established by the prestige with which the Roman Church was held throughout the West, as well as its formal adoption by the Carolingians wherever Frankish power extended. Thus, whether Frank or Anglo-Saxon, Roman or German, the Christians of the Dark Ages found a principle of unity in the Latin liturgy—a unity that bound them not only religiously across various lands and cultures but also temporally, providing a vital connection to the earliest ages of Christianity.

The Church emerged from antiquity and created a new world on the ruins of a fallen empire. That world both reflected and further defined the values of the Christian faith, and the mission of Christ to the whole world. Anyone who follows the history of the Church into the succeeding centuries will clearly see how the presumed "darkness" of this era was more accurately a new dawn, and how the many seeds planted during the Dark Ages blossomed into the full flower of the High Middle Ages.

Notes

1. Our Roman Heritage

1. Edict of Thessalonica, *Codex Theodosianus*, xvi.1.2 (https://en.wikipedia.org/wiki/Edict_of_Thessalonica).

2. Irenaeus, *Against Heresies*, book III, chap. 3.

3. St. Cyprian to Pope Cornelius, letter. *The Complete Works of St. Cyprian of Carthage*, ed. Phillip Campbell (Merchantville, NJ: Arx Publishing, 2013), letter 44.

2. The Church among Gauls and Goths

1. *Encyclopaedia Britannica*, 11th ed. (1911), s.v. "Hilarius, St."

2. St. Cyprian of Carthage, letter 53.

3. Gregory of Tours, *Historia Francorum*, Book II:30.

4. Johann Laurence Mosheim, *Ecclesiastical History Ancient and Modern*, vol. 1 (New York: Harpers Brothers, 1856), 132.

3. The Age of St. Benedict

1. Gregory I, *Dialogues of Pope Gregory the Great*, book II, chap. 1. https://www.osb.org/gen/greg/.

2. Leonard J. Doyle, *St. Benedict's Rule for Monasteries* (Collegeville, MN: St. John's Abbey Press, 1948), chap. 1.

3. *St. Benedict's Rule*, chap. 1.

4. *St. Benedict's Rule*, chap. 2.

5. *St. Benedict's Rule*, chap. 7.

6. *St. Benedict's Rule*, chap. 48.

7. Benedict XVI, General Audience, Apr. 9, 2008. http://www.vatican.va/content/benedict-xvi/en/audiences/2008/documents/hf_ben-xvi_aud_20080409.html.

4. Missionary Monks

1. This maxim of Belloc is found elaborated in his book *Europe and the Faith* (New York: Paulist Press, 1920).

2. St. Patrick, *Confession*, chap. 16. https://www.confessio.ie/#.

3. Venerable Bede, Historia ecclesiastica gentis Anglorum, *Ecclesiastical History of the English Church and People* (London: Penguin Classics, 1991) book 25.

4. *Historia ecclesiastica gentis Anglorum*, book 3, chap. 25.

155

5. The Church of Rome

1. Irenaeus, *Against Heresies*, book III, chap. 3.

2. "The Edict of Valentinian III," ed. Henry Bettenson, *Documents of the Early Christian Church* (Oxford University Press, 1967), 22–23.

3. "Acts of the Council of Chalcedon," ed. Philip Schaff, *Nicene and Post-Nicene Fathers*, series 2, vol. 14. (Grand Rapids, MI: Eerdmans, 1899), session II.

4. Second Vatican Council, *Constitution on the Sacred Liturgy Sacrosanctum Concilium*, 116. https://www.vatican.va/archive/hist_councils/ii_vatican_council/documents/vat-ii_const_19631204_sacrosanctum-concilium_en.html.

5. Paul the Deacon, "Life of Pope Gregory the Great," XV, quoted in Huddleston, *The Catholic Encyclopedia*, s.v. "Pope Gregory I ('the Great')" (New York: Robert Appleton Company, 1909). Retrieved April 22, 2021, from New Advent: http://www.newadvent.org/cathen/06780a.htm.

6. Gregory the Great, epistle 13:50 and 5:154, quoted in Huddleston, *The Catholic Encyclopedia*, s. v. "Pope Gregory I ('the Great')" (New York: Robert Appleton Company, 1909). Retrieved April 22, 2021, from New Advent: http://www.newadvent.org/cathen/06780a.htm.

7. Cyprian of Carthage, On the Unity of the Church, ed. Phillip Campbell, *The Complete Works of St. Cyprian of Carthage* (Merchantville, NJ: Arx Publishing, 2013), section 4.

8. Prosper of Aquitaine, "Epitoma Chronica" for the year 452, source from the accounts translated in J. H. Robinson, *Readings in European History* (Boston: Ginn, 1905), 49–51. https://sourcebooks.fordham.edu/source/attila2.asp.

9. "Epitoma Chronica."

6. East and West

1. "First Council of Constantinople: 381," Papal Encyclicals Online, accessed April 15, 2021, https://www.papalencyclicals.net.

2. Leo the Great, letter 106, trans. Charles Lett Feltoe, *Nicene and Post-Nicene Fathers*, Second Series, vol. 12, ed. Philip Schaff and Henry Wace (Buffalo, NY: Christian Literature Publishing Co., 1895).

3. Gregory I, *Dialogues*, book IX, letter 59.

4. *Dialogues*, book IX, letter 12.

5. *Dialogues*, book VII, letter 40.

6. *Dialogues*, book VII, letter 40.

7. Second Council of Nicaea, session VII, October 13, 787. https://www.newworldencyclopedia.org/entry/Second_Council_of_Nicaea.

8. Opuscula 11, PG 91.137–140, trans. Cooper 2005:181, *The Oxford Handbook of Maximus the Confessor*, ed. Pauline Allen and Bronwen Neil (Oxford University Press, 2015).

9. Gregory I, *Dialogues*, book IX, letter 12.

10. Dom Chapman, J. (1923), *Studies on the Early Papacy* (Sheed & Ward; London), pp 213–214.

7. The Carolingian Renaissance

1. Kampers, *The Catholic Encyclopedia*, s. v. "Pepin the Short," (New York: Robert Appleton Company, 1911). Retrieved April 22, 2021, from New Advent: http://www .newadvent.org/cathen/11662b.htm.

2. Heinrich Fichtenau, "The Carolingian Empire," *Studies in Medieval History*, vol. 9, trans. Peter Munz, ed. Geoffrey Barraclough (Oxford, UK: Basil Blackwell, 1963), 47–48.

3. Einhard, "Life of Charlemagne," chap. 27.

4. Einhard, "Life of Charlemagne," chap. 24.

5. William Turner, "Carolingian Schools," *The Catholic Encyclopedia*, vol. 3 (New York: Robert Appleton, 1908), http://www.newadvent.org.

6. "Carolingian Schools."

7. "Carolingian Schools."

8. John Damascene, *Fountain of Knowledge*, 99–116, quoted in St. John of Damascus, *Writings*, vol. 37 (Washington, DC: Catholic University of America Press, 1958), pp. 153–160.

8. Imperium and Sacerdotium

1. Asser, *Life of King Alfred*, trans. L. C. Jane (New York: Cooper Square, 1966), 56, 82.

2. *Life of King Alfred*, 56.

3. *Life of King Alfred*, 26–27.

4. *Life of King Alfred*, 49.

9. Sacramental Controversies

1. Augustine, *The Good of Marriage*, 24, trans. C.L. Cornish, *Nicene and Post-Nicene Fathers*, First Series, vol. 3, ed. Philip Schaff (Buffalo, NY: Christian Literature Publishing Co., 1887). Revised and edited for New Advent by Kevin Knight. http://www .newadvent.org/fathers/1309.htm.

2. "Penitential of Cummean," English translation based on John T. McNeill and Helena M. Gamer, "Medieval Handbooks of Penance: A Translation of the Principal

Libri Poenitentiales and Selections from Related Documents," *Records of Civilization Sources and Studies*, no. 29 (New York: Columbia University Press, 1938), 98–117.

3. Ignatius of Antioch, Letter to Smyrna, 7, trans. Alexander Roberts and James Donaldson, ed. Alexander Roberts, James Donaldson, and A. Cleveland Coxe, *Ante-Nicene Fathers*, vol. 1, ed. Alexander Roberts, James Donaldson, and A. Cleveland Coxe (Buffalo, NY: Christian Literature Publishing Co., 1885). Revised and edited for New Advent by Kevin Knight. http://www.newadvent.org/fathers/0109.htm.

10. The Cluniac Reform

1. Lucy Margaret Smith, *The Early History of the Monastery of Cluny* (Oxford University Press 1920), 11–12.

2. See Christian Cochini, *The Apostolic Origins of Priestly Celibacy*, preface by Alfons M. Stickler, trans. Nelly Marans (San Francisco: Ignatius Press, 1990).

3. Origin, Homily 23, *Homilies on Numbers* (Downers Grove, IL: Intervarsity Press, 2009).

4. Council of Elvira, *Apostolic Origins of Priestly Celibacy*, sect. 33.

Index

abbots, 37
Acacius, 76–77
Adelman, 130
Adrian I, Pope, 82
Africa (Petrarch), xx
Alaric, 3, 24
Alcuin, 93–94, 101, 129
Alemanni, 22
Alfred, 108–112
Ambrose, St., 2, 17, 56
Anastasius (antipope), 113
anchorites, 36
Anglo-Saxons, 50–51, 109, 112
Annales Ecclesiastici (Baronius), xxi
Anskar, St., 57
Arius, 13
Arles, Council of, 12
Arnulf, 113
Ashdown, Battle of, 110
Asser, 108, 110, 111
Athanasius, 73
Attila the Hun, 7, 21, 51, 70–71
Augustine, St., 50–51, 54
Augustine of Hippo, St., 2, 13–14, 18–20,
    21, 118
    City of God, The, 3–4, 93
    Soliloquies, 111
Augustus, 4, 73
Aurelius of Milan, 19

Baptism, 120, 122
barbarian invasions, 61–62
Baronius, Caesar, xxi
Bede, St., 52–53
Belloc, Hilaire, 45
Benedict III, Pope, 113
Benedict IX, Pope, 115, 145, 147
Benedict XVI, Pope, 42
Benedict of Aniane, St., 95, 96
Benedict of Nursia, St.
    Abbey of Monte Cassino, 34
    death, 42
    Dialogues (Gregory), 31, 32
    education, 30–31
    influence of, 29, 42–43

Rule of, 33, 36–40, 94–95, 142–143
sieve miracle, 31–32
at Subiaco, 33–34
Berengar, 128–136
Berno, St., 140–141, 142–143
Bertha, 50
bishops, appointment of, 102–104, 105–106
Boniface, St., 55–57, 103
Brendan, St., 48
Brigid, St., 49
Britain, 49–51, 54
Byzantine Empire, 10, 63, 83, 89, 91. *See also*
    Eastern churches

Cadaver Synod, 113, 115
canon law, 8
cappa Sancti Martini (cloak of St. Martin),
    14–15
Carolingian era
    Charlemagne's reign, 90–97
    educational reforms, 93–94
    end of, 97–98
    Eucharistic controversies, 124–129
    importance of, 98–99
    monastic reforms, 94–95
    Roman Rite, 95–97
Carolingians, 89–92
Cassiodorus, 63
Catholic Church. *See also* Eastern churches
    canon law, 8
    corruption in, 145–146
    disputes with Constantinople, 75–76
    influence of, 101
    Latin language in, 7–8
    lay domination in, 112–115, 139–140,
        146–148
    liturgical rites, 96–97, 151
    papacy, 6–7
    primacy of Rome, 59–61
    rise of, 4–5
    secular influence on, 105–106
    theological continuity, 151–153
Celestine, Pope, 21, 46, 47
celibacy, 68, 105, 146, 148–150
Cenobites, 36

chant, 65, 97
Charlemagne, 14, 91–97, 98, 101, 104, 107, 111
Charles Martel, 55, 89, 99–100, 103, 104
Charles the Bald, 97–98, 125–126
Charles the Fat, 97
Charles the Simple, 97
City of God, The (Augustine), 3–4, 93
Clement I, Pope, 70
Clotilde, 22
Clovis, 21–23, 26, 89
Cluniac reforms, 142–148, 149–150
Cluny Abbey, 139–141
Colman, St., 52–53
Columba, St., 48, 49
commendatory system, 102
confession, 119–123
Confession (Patrick), 47
Conleth, 49
Constans II, 84
Constantine, 4–5, 15
Constantine V Copronymous, 82
Constantius Chlorus, 12
Constantius II, 13
Copernicus, Nicolaus, 58
councils. See ecumenical councils
Crusades, 98, 99–100
Cummean, 123
Cyprian, St., 7, 19, 69, 124
Cyril, St., 53–54, 57

Damasus, Pope, 6, 75
Dark Ages, origins of term, xix–xxiii
Dawkins, Richard, 40
De Corpore et Sanguine Domine (Pachasius), 125
Decius, 4
Denis, St., 12
Dialogues (Gregory), 31, 32
Diocletian, 4, 10, 12, 17
Divine Office, 39, 144–145
Donation of Pepin, 90
Druids, 46
Druthmar, Christian, 125

Easter, date of, 52–53
Eastern churches
    Acacian Schism, 76–77, 87
    acknowledgement of primacy of Rome, 87
    Constantinople, 74–76
    disputes with Rome, 75–76
    ecumenical patriarch title controversy, 79–80
    Great Schism of 1054, 86
    iconoclasm, 80–83
    Photian Schism, 85–86
    Three Chapters controversy, 77–79
ecumenical councils
    Arles, 12
    Béziers, 13
    Carthage, 6
    Chalcedon, 6, 61–62, 76–77
    Constantinople, 75
    Constantinople, Second, 78
    Elvira, 150
    Ephesus, 5–6
    Hiera, 83
    Lateran, 84
    Lateran, Fourth, 119, 133, 136–137
    Nicaea, 24
    Nicaea, Second, 82–83
    Orange, Second, 21
    Orleans, Fifth, 104
    Paris, Third, 104
    Rome, 6, 132
    Tours, 132
    Vatican, Second, 65
    Vercelli, 131
Edict of Milan, 4–5
education, 40–41, 93–94, 109–110
Eilmer of Malmesbury, 58
Einhard, 92–93
Enda, St., 48–49
England. See Britain
Enlightenment, xxi–xxii
Eriugena, John Scotus, 126, 130
Essay on the Development of Doctrine (Newman), 134
Ethelbert, 50–51
Ethelred, 110
Eucharist
    Berengar's heresy, 128–136
    controversies, 124–129
    doctrine, 134–137

transubstantiation, 129, 133, 134, 136–137
Eulogius, 79–80
Eusebius, 131–132, 150

Fanchea, St., 48
Felix III, Pope, 63, 76–77
Finnian, St., 49
Flavian, St., 61
Fleury Abbey, 143–144
Florus Magister, 125
Formosus, Pope, 113, 115
Formula of Hormisdas (John II), 87
Fountain of Knowledge, The (John of Damascus), 99
Franks, 21–24, 96, 104. *See also* Carolingians
Frederick II, xxi
Fulbert, 129

Gallic Wars (Julius Caesar), 41
Gallo-Romans, 12
Gaul, 11–12, 60, 96
Gelasius I, Pope, 62, 69
Geoffrey II, 131
Germain, St., 47
Germany, 54–57
Gibbon, Edward, xxii, 9
Glagolitic alphabet, 53
Golden Legend (Jacopo de Voraigne), 17
Goths, 23–24. *See also* Ostrogoths; Visigoths
Gratian, John, 147
Great Persecution, 4–5, 12, 17
Gregorian chant, 65, 97
Gregorian reforms, 149–150
Gregory I, Pope
	acknowledgement of primacy of Rome, 87
	as biographer of St. Benedict, 3, 32, 34
	death, 68
	Dialogues, 3, 32
	early years, 63–64
	ecumenical patriarch title controversy, 79–80
	Liber Pastoralis Curae, 66
	Pastoral Care, 111
	pontificate, 64–65, 66–69
	and St. Augustine, 50, 54
	on St. Hermengild, 25
Gregory II, Pope, 55

Gregory III, Pope, 81, 103
Gregory VI, Pope, 147
Gregory VII, Pope, 127, 148, 149
Gregory Nazianzus, St., 73
Gregory of Tours, 22, 25, 129
Guthrum, 110
Guy of Spoleto, 113

Hadrian, Pope, 96
Hadrianum, 96
Haimo, 125
Haüy, René-Just, 58
Helen, St., 12
Henotikon (Acacius), 76
Henri I, 131
Henry III, 147
heresies
	Arianism, 13, 23–26
	Berengar's, 128–136
	iconoclasm, 80–83
	Monophysitism, 6, 61–62, 64, 76, 77–78
	Monothelitism, 84–85
	Nestorianism, 5, 77
	Pelagianism, 18–21
	trilinguistic, 53
Hermengild, St., 25
Hibernicus, 92
Hilary of Arles, St., 18, 21, 60–61
Hilary of Poitiers, St., 12–14, 16, 26
Hildebert, 134
Hildebrand, 146–148
Hincmar, 125, 126
Hispanian Church, 24–25
historiography, xix–xx
History of the Decline and Fall of the Roman Empire (Gibbon), xxii
History of the English Church and People (Bede), 52–53
Holy Roman Empire, 104–108
Hormisdas, Pope, 77
Hosius of Cordoba, 24
Hugues, 130
humility, 38
Hypostatic Union, 6

iconoclasm, 80–83
Ignatius, Patriarch, 85
Ignatius of Antioch, St., 137
inculturation, 46

indulgences, 123–124
Innocent I, Pope, 19
Investiture Controversy, 108, 115
Ireland, 46–49
Irenaeus, St., 7, 59
Irene, 82–83
Isidore, St., 25–26, 101
Islam, 99–100

Jacopo de Voraigne, 17
John II, Patriarch, 87
John II, Pope, 62, 69
John VIII, Pope, 86
John X, Pope, 114, 143
John XI, Pope, 114
John XII, Pope, 104, 107, 115
John Chrysostom, St., 73
John Henry Newman, St., 134
John of Cappadocia, 77
John of Damascus, St., 99
John Paul II, Pope, 54
John the Faster, 79–80
Joseph II, 57
Julius Caesar, 12, 41
Justin I, 77
Justinian I, 63, 77–78

Killian, St., 55

Lambert, 113
land grants, 102, 112, 139–140
Lanfranc, 130–131, 132
Latin language, 7–8, 151
Leander, St., 25–26
Leo I, Pope, 7, 59–62, 69, 70–71, 75–76
Leo III, 81
Leo III, Pope, 91, 107
Leo V, 83
Leo IX, Pope, 131, 147
Liber Pastoralis Curae (Gregory), 66
literacy, 40–41
Liturgy of the Hours, 39, 144–145
Liuvigild, 25–26
Livy, 41
Loman, St., 48
Lombards, 89–90
Louis II, 113
Louis the Pious, 95, 97
Louis the Stammerer, 97–98

Luther, Martin, xx–xxi

MacCarthem, St., 48
manuscript copying, 41
Marcus Aurelius, 4
marriage, 118–119
Martin I, Pope, 84
Martin, St., 14–15, 20, 26, 34, 47, 51, 129
Marx, Karl, 40
Marzonia, 114
Maximus, 17
Maximus the Confessor, St., 84–85
Mel, St., 48, 49
Mendel, Gregor, 58
Merovech, 21
Merovingians, 14, 21, 89–90, 104
Methodius, St., 53–54, 57
Michael III, 85
Middle Ages, prejudices against, xx–xxi
Milchu, 47
Monica, St., 2
monks and monastic life
    abbots, 37
    in Britain, 49–51, 54
    Carolingian reforms, 94–95
    Cenobites, 36
    choir monks, 144–145
    Cluniac reforms, 142–148
    commendatory system, 102, 139
    contributions of, 57–58
    crises in, 141–142
    educational reforms, 93–94
    in Germany, 54–57
    in Ireland, 46–49
    manuscript copying, 41
    missionary work of, 45–53, 57
    ora et labora (prayer and work)
        philosophy, 38–40, 144–145
    Rule of St. Benedict, 36–40
    virtues of, 37–38
Monte Cassino, Abbey of, 34

Nestorius, 5
New Testament canon, 6
Nicholas, Pope, 85–86
Normans, 98, 112

Odo, St., 143–144, 149
Odoacer, 1–2, 5, 30

On the Advantage of Death (Ambrose), 56
ora et labora (prayer and work) philosophy, 38–40, 144–145
Origen, 149
original sin, 18–20
Ostrogoths, 24, 30, 35, 63
Oswiu, 52–53
Otto I, 104–108
"Our Lady's Psalter," 144

Paeda, 51
paganism, 4–5, 16–17, 21, 45–46, 49–51, 54–56, 85, 100
Palladius, St., 46
papacy
    importance of, 6–7, 62–63
    infallibility, 115–116
    "Ottonian privilege," 106–108
    Patrimony of St. Peter, 63, 67–68
    primacy of Rome, 59–61, 68–70, 87
    Saeculum obscurum (Dark Age), 112–116
    vicars, 62
Papal States, 90, 100
Paschasius Radbertus, St., 125–128, 130, 133, 135
Pastoral Care (Gregory), 111
Patrick, St., 17, 46–48, 49
Patrimony of St. Peter, 63, 67–68, 147
Paul, St., 7, 18–19, 38, 69, 73
Pax Romana, 4, 73
peace movements, 144
Pelagius, 18–19
Pelagius II, Pope, 64
penance, 120–123. *See also* indulgences
Pepin, 56, 89–90, 96–97
persecution, 4–5, 12, 17, 81, 82
Peter, St., 5, 7, 59, 60, 69
Peter Damian, St., 149
Petrarch, xx
Photius, 85–86
Pius IX, Pope, 14
prayers and praying
    Divine Office/Liturgy of the Hours, 39, 144–145
    "Our Lady's Psalter," 144
Priscillian, 17
Prosper, St., 18, 21, 71

Protestant Reformation, xx–xxi, 108

Rabanus Maurus, 125
Ratramnus, 125–126, 129, 131–132, 133
Reccared, 26, 101
rectors, 67–68
regents, 114–115
Remigius, St., 22–23, 26
Rollo, 98
Roman Empire
    Christianity as official religion of, 5, 17
    civic life of, 40–41
    culture of, 7–8, 11
    Eastern, 7, 10, 63, 74–75
    fall of, xxii, 1–3, 7, 9–10, 62
    unity of, 73–74
Roman Rite, 95–97, 151
Romanus, 33
Rome, primacy of, 59–61, 68–70, 87
Romulus Agustulus, 1–2, 5
Rudolf, 143
Rule of St. Benedict, 36–40, 94–95

sacraments
    baptism, 120, 122
    confession, 119–123
    Eucharistic controversies, 124–134
    Eucharistic doctrine, 134–137
    ex opera operato manner of effects, 136
    in genera, 117
    marriage, 118–119
    in specie, 117
Saturninus, 13
Scholastica, St., 33, 42
scriptoriums, 41
Sergius III, Pope, 114
Silvia, St., 63
simony, 145
Simplicius, Pope, 62, 69
sin, original, 18–20
Sixtus III, Pope, 60
Soliloquies (Augustine), 111
Song of Roland, 98, 111
Stephen II, Pope, 90
Stephen VI, Pope, 113, 115
Sylvester I, Pope, 24
Sylvester II, Pope, 126
Sylvester III, Pope, 147
synods, 23, 60, 81, 109

Cadaver, 113, 115
Carthage, 19
Elvira, 24
Numidia, 19
Rome, 8
Sutri, 147
Toledo, 24
Whitby, 52–53

Tertullian, 124, 150
Theodoric, 30, 62
Theodosius I, 5, 73
Theophylactus, 114
Three Chapters controversy, 77–79
Tome of Leo, 61
Totila, 35
translatio imperii, 91
transubstantiation, 129, 133, 134, 136–137

Urban II, Pope, 100

Valentine, Basil, 58
Valentinian, 13
Valentinian III, 60
Verdun, Treaty of, 97, 104
Vigilius, Pope, 78–79
Vikings, 97–98, 142, 143
virtues, 37–38
Visigoths, 24–26, 30, 62, 78
Voltaire, xxi–xxii

Walafrid Strabo, 125
Wilfrid, St., 52–53
William I, 139–141, 142
Willibrord, St., 55
Witiza, 95
women, status of, 119
Wynfrith, 54–55

Zachary, Pope, 90
Zeno, 76
Zosimus, Pope, 19

Phillip Campbell is an author of several books, including *Story of the Church*, and the four-volume Story of Civilization series. He has also contributed to and edited a number of books and wrote two history textbooks. He is an instructor at Homeschool Connections and previously served two terms as mayor of Howell, Michigan.

Campbell has a bachelor's degree in European history from Ave Maria University and a certificate in secondary education from Madonna University. Campbell has appeared on EWTN television, Ave Maria Radio, Radio Maria, Good Shepherd Catholic Radio, Mater Dei Radio, and on the Crawford Broadcasting Network.

Campbell and his children live in southern Michigan.

www.phillipcampbell.net

Facebook: Phillip Campbell, Author-Teacher

YouTube: Mr. Campbell Explains

The Reclaiming
CATHOLIC HISTORY SERIES

The history of the Catholic Church is often clouded by myth, misinformation, and missing pieces. Today there is a renewed interest in recovering the true history of the Church, correcting the record in the wake of centuries of half-truths and noble lies. Books in the Reclaiming Catholic History series, edited by Mike Aquilina and written by leading authors and historians, bring Church history to life, debunking the myths one era at a time.

Titles in the Series Include:

The Early Church

The Church and the Roman Empire

The Church and the Dark Ages

The Church and the Middle Ages

The Church and the Age of Reformations

The Church and the Age of Enlightenment

The Church and the Modern Era

**Look for titles in this series wherever books and eBooks are sold.
Visit avemariapress.com for more information.**